Drugs and the Law

ISSUES

Volume 62

Editor

Craig Donnellan

 *Independence*

First published by Independence
PO Box 295
Cambridge CB1 3XP
England

British Library Cataloguing in Publication Data
Drugs and the Law – (Issues Series)
I. Donnellan, Craig II. Series
362.2'9'0941

ISBN 1 86168 238 7

Printed in Great Britain
MWL Print Group Ltd

Typeset by
Claire Boyd

Cover
The illustration on the front cover is by
Pumpkin House.

CONTENTS

Chapter One: Drug Misuse

Chapter Two: Drugs and the Law

Introduction

Drugs and the Law is the sixty-second volume in the **Issues** series. The aim of this series is to offer up-to-date information about important issues in our world.

Drugs and the Law examines drug misuse and the legalisation debate.

The information comes from a wide variety of sources and includes:
Government reports and statistics
Newspaper reports and features
Magazine articles and surveys
Web site material
Literature from lobby groups
and charitable organisations.

It is hoped that, as you read about the many aspects of the issues explored in this book, you will critically evaluate the information presented. It is important that you decide whether you are being presented with facts or opinions. Does the writer give a biased or an unbiased report? If an opinion is being expressed, do you agree with the writer?

Drugs and the Law offers a useful starting-point for those who need convenient access to information about the many issues involved. However, it is only a starting-point. At the back of the book is a list of organisations which you may want to contact for further information.

*****

Young make drugs part of everyday life

Employed users challenge idea of 'losers' funding habit by crime

Britain's twentysomethings have defined their own 'sensible' drug-taking culture and incorporated a regular use of illegal substances into a work hard/play hard lifestyle, according to research.

Far from 'maturing out' of adolescent binge drinking and occasional drug taking, these young people are helping to make recreational drug use part of everyday life.

They are also challenging assumptions that drug users are unemployed and unemployable people who could only fund their habit through crime.

Howard Parker and a research team at Manchester University have monitored hundreds of young people in north-west England since they were aged 13 or 14. The team warned yesterday that the government's drug strategy must incorporate tobacco and, especially, alcohol use, and embrace the 'realities' of how people actually behaved.

'In the absence of any public health messages for young adults into their lifestyles, hard-soft drug distinctions are becoming increasingly blurred.

'At 18, nearly all this group said they would never touch cocaine because it was addictive. Yet by 23, more than a quarter of them have used cocaine powder.'

This research coincides with a separate survey which found that increasing numbers of teenagers are using cannabis.

The proportion of 14- and 15-year-old boys who said they had tried the drug jumped from 19% in 1999, to 29% in 2001, according to research by the schools health education unit. Cannabis, which is being down-graded from a Class B to a Class C

By James Meikle, Health Correspondent

---

drug, was the only illegal drug not considered to be 'always unsafe' by older children, the unit found.

Researchers said that the response of 22- to 23-year-olds indicated few signs of moderation since they were 18.

Far from 'maturing out' of adolescent binge drinking and occasional drug taking, these young people are helping to make recreational drug use part of everyday life

---

At 18, 82% were weekly drinkers; most went drinking several times a week. This profile was almost identical five years later. Binge drinking remained endemic.

At 18, 63% of the sample had tried an illegal drug. By 23, this had risen to 76%.

Professor Parker, director of Manchester University's social policy applied research centre, said: 'Even now, more than half remain drug active with 30% being regular drug users (having tried at least one drug in the last month), primarily of cannabis, followed by ecstasy and now cocaine replacing amphetamine and LSD use.'

As he and fellow researchers reported in the journal *Sociology*: 'Thus far, their drug involvement is only plateauing and at a high rate. It is only with their increasing tendency to become cannabis users despite

previous, more florid, drug repertoires, that these users are showing signs of moderation.'

The young people said their parents, too, were far more 'realistic' and tolerant of cannabis use than they were a few years ago.

Prof Parker explained yesterday: 'What has changed is the way their substance abuse is managed.

'Subjects reported they now exercised more self-discipline and control over their drug use and binge drinking, by restricting it far more to weekends.

'The sample see their substance use as de-stressing – chilling out activity, whereby intoxicated weekends and going out to "get out of it" is the antidote to the working week.'

Access to drugs was straightforward, according to the article in *Sociology.*

Educated, employed, and otherwise conforming young people had informal drugs distribution methods whereby friends and friends of friends 'sorted' the matter, distancing them from 'real' dealers.

Their choice of drugs, beyond cannabis, was partly determined by the need to get up for work on weekdays. Thus cocaine powder, which, for most, had short-term effects, was replacing LSD and amphetamines.

There were other limits on 'sensible' consumption. Both drug users and abstainers were less comfortable with friends who regularly took Class A drugs such as cocaine, ecstasy, heroin, and LSD.

'What the Class A stimulant users have done is pose a very knotty political dilemma.

'As primarily educated, employed young citizens with otherwise conforming profiles, they challenge the "war on drugs" discourse which prefers to link drug use with crime and personal tragedy and utilises this discourse as a reason for not calling a truce.'

© *Guardian Newspapers Limited 2002*

Drugs identification guide

Information from the Metropolitan Police

Amphetamines – 'Speed' 'Uppers' 'Whizz' 'Sulph'

Possible physical effects
- Increased alertness, nervous excitability and energy.
- Increased pulse rate, loss of appetite.
- Followed by low of irritability, depression and tiredness.
- Can lead to long-term psychosis.

What to look for
- Can be injected.
- Most often found in brightly coloured tablet or powder form.

The law
Class B Drug

Cannabis – 'Pot' 'Grass' 'Puff' 'Weed' 'Spliff'

Possible physical effects
- Relaxed inhibitions, talkativeness, excitability.
- Large doses: lethargy, confusion, disorientation, paranoia and panic.
- Even small amounts can affect learning ability and skills such as driving.
- Cannabis is harmful to health.

What to look for
- Strong sweet sickly smell when smoked.
- Cigarette ends made from rolled cards.
- Herbal and resinous substances.
- Small plastic packages, homemade pipes.

The law
Class B Drug

Cocaine – 'Coke' 'Charlie' 'Snow' 'Crack'

Possible physical effects
- Short-term feeling of intense pleasure.
- Often followed with rebound effect of moodiness and depression.
- An increased heart rate and blood pressure.
- Pupils dilated.
- Can be associated with eating disorders.
- Can be injected, smoked or sniffed.

What to look for
- Needles, syringes, straws, homemade pipes and water coolers.
- White powder, small quantities of broken white 'marble like' substance.

The law
Class A Drug

Ecstasy – 'E's' 'Doves' 'Rhubarb & Custard' 'Disco burgers'

Possible physical effects
- Rush similar to amphetamine.
- Feeling of well-being and friendship, panic and depression.
- Often used in the rave dance scene to remove inhibitions and increase energy.
- Can lead to heatstroke and extreme thirst.
- Deaths through use are being recorded.

What to look for
- Powder, tablet or capsule form.
- Much of the Ecstasy sold is adulterated with other drugs.

The law
Class A Drug

Hallucinogens – 'LSD' 'Acid' 'Tabs' 'Magic Mushrooms'

Possible physical effects
- Heightened sensory appreciation, illusions, hallucinations and disorientation.
- It can be either pleasant or extremely disturbing.
- Can take the form of an 'out of body' experience.
- 'Flashback' experiences may occur over a period of time.

What to look for
- Small paper squares, often with printed designs such as strawberries, cartoon or cult characters.
- Microdot tablets, small mushrooms.

The law
Class A Drug

Heroin – 'Smack' 'Scag' 'Gear' 'H'

Possible physical effects
- Euphoria followed by drowsiness and contentment.
- Reduced reaction to pain and discomfort.
- An addictive drug.
- Long term: self-neglect and poor personal hygiene, loss of appetite, watery eyes, running nose, sores and needle marks.

What to look for
- Burnt foil or spoons.
- Hypodermic syringes and needles.
- Brown powders or green liquid (Methadone).

The law
Class A Drug

Other misused drugs – 'Downers' 'Bennies' Pills

Prescribed medicines (including barbiturates, tranquillisers, anabolic steroids, sleeping pills and painkillers) are commonly misused, as are solvents and gases.

Possible physical effects
- Changing behaviour varying according to type and intended use of drug.
- Solvents and gases are immediate in effect. Extreme 'drunkenness', disorientation, blank expression, chemical smell on breath, impairment of mental and physical state.

What to look for
- Prescribed medicines disappearing.
- Containers for glues, aerosols, cleaning fluids etc.
- Plastic bags used for inhaling.

The law
Prescribed medicines range from class A, B, to C. Solvents and gases are not for sale to under-18s.

- The above information is from the Metropolitan Police's web site which can be found at www.met.police.uk

© *Metropolitan Police*

How many drugs are seized by customs and the police?

Every year HM Customs and Excise intercept hundreds of shipments or people bringing illicit drugs into the country. The police seize drugs already in the country, either smuggled, grown or made here. The number and quantity of these seizures are recorded and published yearly by the Home Office in the form of statistical bulletins.

While the bulletins show what drugs are being reported and seized at the ports and on the streets, they reveal more about the activities of customs and the police than they do about what is actually available.

The tables show what was seized recently by customs and police. Though the police appear to have made more seizures (hence arrests), these tend to be smaller quantities. Custom seizures, on the other hand, tend to be much larger, hence them finding greater quantities of drugs – except for cannabis plants, which are increasingly being homegrown in the UK.

- The above information is from DrugScope's web site which can be found at www.drugscope.org.uk

© *DrugScope*

Total number of seizures made by customs and police 1994 to 1999 in the UK

1999	5,209	126,985	132,194
1998	7,753	143,966	151,719
1997	6,727	132,447	139,174
1996	7,949	114,170	122,119
1995	6,844	107,695	114,539
1994	7,187	100,442	107,629

Quantity seized (kg or units/doses*) in UK by customs and police according to drug type in 1999

Drug type	Customs	Police	Total
Cocaine	2,485	471	2,956
Crack	1.7	14.5	16.1
Heroin	848	1,494	2,342
LSD*	40,962	26,446	67,408
Ecstasy*	4,825,421	1,498,048	6,323,469
Herbal cannabis	14,279	1,588	15,867
Cannabis plants*	11	55,352	55,363
Cannabis resin	40,636	12,374	53,010
Amphetamines	1,118	899	2,017

Value at street prices (£) of main drug types seized by UK police and customs in 1999

Drug type	Customs	Police	Total
Cocaine	156,573	29,690	186,264
Crack	165	1,446	1,611
Heroin	55,120	97,093	152,214
LSD	159	102	260
Ecstasy	53,080	16,479	69,558
Herbal cannabis	44,825	4,986	49,811
Cannabis resin	143,337	43,647	186,985
Amphetamines	11,176	8,989	20,165
All main drugs	464,435	202,432	666,868

Drug use among young people in England

By the National Centre for Social Research/National Foundation for Educational Research

Summary

This article gives preliminary results from a major national survey of secondary school children aged 11-15 published by the Department of Health. The survey was carried out by the National Centre for Social Research (NatCen) and the National Foundation for Educational Research (NFER) among more than 9,300 pupils in 285 schools in England in the autumn of 2001 for the Home Office and the Department of Health. Among the survey's key findings are that, in 2001:

- 12 per cent of pupils had used drugs in the last month and 20 per cent had used drugs in the last year;
- 10 per cent of pupils aged 11-15 were regular smokers, the same proportion as in 2000;
- The proportion of pupils who drank in the last week had increased to 26 per cent from 24 per cent in 2000.

Drug use

One of the key performance indicators in the government's 10-year strategy for tackling drug misuse is 'To reduce the proportion of people under the age of 25 reporting use of Class A drugs by 25 per cent by 2005 and 50 per cent by 2008'. The key survey measures are the proportions of pupils who have used drugs (including particular Class A drugs) in the last month and the last year.

A revised method of measuring prevalence of taking or using drugs was introduced in 2001. The questions used in 2001 provide new estimates of drug use and are not strictly comparable with results from previous surveys, although it is likely that drug use either stayed the same or increased slightly between 2000 and 2001. Thirteen categories of individual drugs are covered in the questionnaire, including cannabis, cocaine, heroin and volatile substances such as gas, glue and other solvents. Combining all categories provides estimates of overall drug use:

- In 2001, 12 per cent of pupils had used drugs in the last month and 20 per cent had used drugs in the last year;
- The proportion of boys taking drugs in the last month (13 per cent) was higher than the proportion of girls (11 per cent), as was the proportion who had used drugs in the last year (21 per cent of boys and 19 per cent of girls);
- There were significant differences by age; in 2001 only 6 per cent of

Prevalence of drug misuse

The extent of drug use among 16- to 59-year-olds. The 2001/2002 *British Crime Survey* estimates that 34% of 16- to 59-year-olds have used an illicit drug at some time and 12% have used a Class A drug. Of all 16- to 59-year-olds, 12% had taken an illicit drug and 3% had used a Class A drug in the last year. This equates to around four million users of any illicit drug and around one million users of Class A drugs.

% used	16-24*	25-34	35-59	16-59	% used	16-24*	25-34	35-59	16-59
Amphetamines					**Tranquillisers**				
Last year	5.0	2.2	0.4	1.6	Last year	1.0	0.6	0.4	0.5
Cannabis					**Amyl nitrate**				
Last year	26.9	13.5	4.1	10.6	Last year	3.8	1.5	0.3	1.2
Cocaine					**Anabolic steroids**				
Last year	4.9	3.3	0.5	2.0	Last year	0.2	0.1	–	0.1
Crack					**Glues**				
Last year	0.5	0.2	0.1	0.2	Last year	0.6	0.1	–	0.1
Ecstasy					**Any drug**				
Last year	6.8	3.1	0.4	2.2	Last year	29.6	15.4	4.9	12.0
Heroin					**Class A**				
Last year	0.3	0.2	0.1	0.2	Last year	8.8	4.9	0.8	3.2
LSD									
Last year	1.2	0.4	–	0.4					
Magic mushrooms									
Last year	1.5	0.7	0.1	0.5					
Methadone									
Last year	–	0.2	–	0.1					

Notes: '–' estimate is less than 0.05%. * Core and boost data

11-year-olds had used drugs in the last year, while 39 per cent of 15-year-olds had done so;

- The pattern of differences according to sex and age has been similar over all four years (1998-2001) of surveys including questions on drugs.

Findings on use of individual drugs include:

- In 2001, cannabis was by far the most likely drug to have been used – 13 per cent of pupils aged 11-15 had used cannabis in the last year. Use of cannabis in the last year was slightly higher among boys (14 per cent) than girls (12 per cent). Cannabis use increased sharply with age: 1 per cent of 11-year-olds had used the drug in the last year compared with 31 per cent of 15-year-olds;
- One per cent of 11- 15-year-olds had used heroin in the last year and 1 per cent had used cocaine. In total, 4 per cent had used Class A drugs in the last year;
- Pupils reported much higher levels of sniffing glue, gas, aerosols or other solvents than they had

in previous years – 7 per cent reported misusing volatile substances in the last year in 2001 compared with 3 per cent in 2000. These new estimates highlight that misuse of volatile substances is more prevalent than previously reported. In general reported levels of use of particular types of drug were similar in 2001 and 2000. This suggests that the higher reported use of volatile substances is primarily a result of the change in question format, rather than a large increase in actual misuse;

- Among 11- and 12-year-olds, misuse of volatile substances in the last year was more common than use of cannabis. Four per cent of 11-year-olds had used volatile substances in the last year and 1 per cent had used cannabis. The equivalent figures for 12-year-olds were 5 per cent and 3 per cent.

Pupils were also asked about which drugs they had been offered in the last year:

- Two-fifths of pupils (42 per cent) had been offered one or more

drugs in the last year. Boys were more likely to have been offered them than were girls (44 per cent compared with 39 per cent);

- As in previous years, cannabis was the drug most likely to have been offered (27 per cent of pupils said they had been offered cannabis) but 22 per cent said they had been offered stimulants (a group of substances which includes cocaine and crack as well as ecstasy, amphetamines and poppers) and 20 per cent that they had been offered glue or gas;
- As with use of drugs, likelihood of having ever been offered drugs increased sharply with age, reaching 66 per cent among 15- year-olds.

- The above information is an extract from the National Centre for Social Research and the National Foundation for Educational Research press notice entitled *Drug use, smoking and drinking among young people in England in 2001.*

Drug misuse

Information from Florence Nightingale Hospitals

Side effects of drug taking

There are physical risks attached to drug taking. These risks arise from the nature of the drug, how much is taken, what the drug is cut with (what the pure form is diluted with), means of delivery and more.

The toxic effects of specific drugs cause short- and long-term effects and damage:

Physical
- Dilated eye pupils
- Bloodshot eyes
- Blurred vision
- Dry mouth and throat, dehydration
- Nausea
- Stomach cramps
- Muscle tension
- Chills
- Sweating
- Blackouts

- Flashbacks
- Increased blood pressure
- Weight loss
- Increased heart rate
- Cardiac arrhythmia/heart problems, heart disease, heart attack
- Seizures
- Respiratory/lung failure
- Lung cancer

Psychological
- Acute psychotic reactions
- Anxiety
- Paranoia
- Personality change

Behavioural
- Mental impairment
- Confusion
- Increased risk of accidents
- Apathy
- Sleeplessness

- Disorientated behaviour, nervous erratic behaviour
- Staring into space
- Hallucinations

Warning signs of drug use
- Constant sniffing
- Sudden irregular mood swings/irritability/anger/hostility
- Sullen uncaring attitude and behaviour

- Gradual loss of interest in hobbies/sport/activities
- Loss of motivation, energy, self-discipline
- Staying out more, possibly in new places/with new people
- Reduced interest in personal grooming/dress and hygiene
- Unhealthy appearance
- Excessive tiredness, change in sleeping patterns
- Use of cologne/deodorants/room air fresheners to hide smells
- Pipes, small boxes or containers, rolling papers or other unusual items.
- Sores and rashes, especially around mouth and nose
- Excessive spending or borrowing of money
- Decline in work/school performance
- Absenteeism, declining work
- Forgetfulness – short or long term
- Loss of appetite
- Trouble with the law

Withdrawal is the body's reaction to the sudden absence of a drug to which it has adapted – this is called 'cold turkey', this physical reaction can last for up to a week. These withdrawal symptoms can range from psychological and physical disruptions ranging from mild anxiety and tremor/shaking to acute psychosis and other more dangerous problems. The effects can be stopped by taking more of the drug.

Drug use patterns

Internal distress, limited life opportunities and unhappiness can predispose an individual to using drugs. The following stages also explain the reasons for the use of drugs further:

Experimental use/contact stage
- Person tries out drugs to satisfy curiosity about their effects, boredom, peer pressure, protest, feel good.
- For many people, drug use stops or remains at this level.

Recreational use stage
- Person uses drugs in a regular pattern over a period of time.

Regular use stage
- Person uses drugs to alter mood in friendly settings and at parties or to be sociable.

Withdrawal is the body's reaction to the sudden absence of a drug to which it has adapted – this is called 'cold turkey', this physical reaction can last for up to a week

---

- Use can be situational (to celebrate or for stress or depression) or spree/binge type.

Excessive use stage
- User spends a great deal of time, energy and money on getting and using one or more drugs.
- Drug use may be solitary or take place in social situations where drug use is the central activity or main reason for the get-together.
- Preoccupation with the quality and effects of drugs becomes noticeable.
- Psychological and physical impairment become apparent.
- Daily functioning is noticeably affected.
- Responsibilities are neglected.
- Relationships with others may become strained and go downhill rapidly.
- Family members (enablers) may find themselves making excuses for the drug user or taking over his or her responsibilities.
- Many heavy drinkers who do not consider themselves alcoholics are in this stage.

Dependent use stage
- Person uses drugs to hold off withdrawal symptoms, which occur after development of physical and psychological dependence. Cold turkey is the name given if rapid withdrawal from drugs takes place.
- Individual's entire perspective for dealing with reality is drug controlled.

Problem drug use tends to refer to drug use which could either be dependent or recreational. It is the effects that drug taking has on the user's life

- This material is for information purposes only and a GP or a qualified professional should be consulted to provide further advice to meet your individual needs. This is not intended to replace qualified medical advice and should not be used to assume a diagnosis. Please consult your GP or a qualified professional to identify a diagnosis and/or commence any type of treatment.

Drug use in Europe and its consequences

What are the main drugs used in the EU today?

Cannabis is the most widely used illicit drug in the EU, followed by amphetamines and ecstasy. Cocaine and LSD are less common, and heroin is only used by a small minority. A tentative extrapolation from recent surveys suggests that at least 45 million Europeans (18% of those aged 15 to 64) have tried cannabis at least once. Of these, around 15 million (about 6% of those aged 15 to 64) have used cannabis in the past 12 months. These proportions are higher among young people. About 25% of those aged 15 to 16 and 40% of those aged 18 have tried cannabis. However, only a minority of those who have taken cannabis use it regularly, and certain legal drugs – such as alcohol, tobacco and some medicines such as tranquillisers – are more widely and more frequently used than any illegal drug.

What is the most harmful drug currently available in the EU?

In almost every EU Member State, the illegal drug associated with the most serious health consequences (in terms of addiction and other problems requiring treatment, drug-related diseases like AIDS or hepatitis, or deaths from overdose) as well as the one with the most serious social problems (such as drug-related crime) is heroin. This is despite the fact that the number of heroin users is only a small proportion of the total population. However, the total number of deaths and diseases related to alcohol and tobacco use are considerably greater than those related to heroin.

How many people die because of illegal drug use in Europe?

Illegal drug use may, in some cases, cause death for various reasons, and different substances imply very different risks. Some deaths (e.g., 'overdoses' or 'acute intoxications') are directly caused by the substances themselves, whereas in many other cases deaths are caused indirectly (e.g., as a result of AIDS acquired by sharing infected injecting equipment). In most cases, national statistics on drug-related deaths refer to deaths directly caused by drug use and are obtained from national mortality registries or from police or forensic records. Deaths indirectly

---

Around 15 million (about 6% of those aged 15 to 64) have used cannabis in the past 12 months

---

caused by drug use are more difficult to identify and compute accurately, but should be taken into account when assessing the public health impact of illicit drug use.

In recent years, according to the EMCDDA's *Annual report on the state of the drugs problem in the European Union*, between six and seven thousand people are recorded annually across the EU as dying from the direct effect of illegal drugs. This figure is almost certainly an underestimate. Furthermore, the figure does not include deaths indirectly related to drug use. The real total of drug-related deaths could therefore be three times higher than the figure given. It should be remembered, however, that alcohol and tobacco use are also related directly or indirectly with a very high number of deaths.

Which substances cause most of these deaths?

In the EU, opiates (especially heroin) are found in most cases of deaths from acute intoxication, but other substances, such as alcohol and benzodiazepines, are often also present. Combining alcohol and benzodiazepines with heroin can

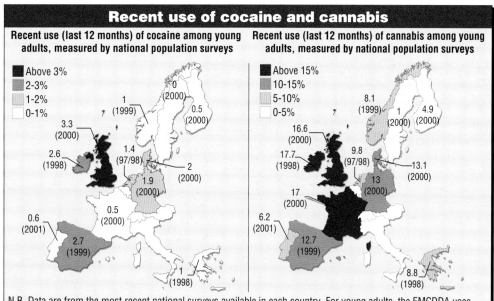

Recent use of cocaine and cannabis

Recent use (last 12 months) of cocaine among young adults, measured by national population surveys

- Above 3%
- 2-3%
- 1-2%
- 0-1%

Recent use (last 12 months) of cannabis among young adults, measured by national population surveys

- Above 15%
- 10-15%
- 5-10%
- 0-5%

N.B. Data are from the most recent national surveys available in each country. For young adults, the EMCDDA uses the range 15-34 years (Denmark and the United Kingdom from 16, Germany and Ireland from 18). Variations in age ranges may slightly influence some national differences. In some countries, the figures were recalculated at a national level to adapt as far as possible to the standard EMCDDA age group.

Source: 2002 Annual report on the state of the drugs problem in the European Union and Norway, EMCDDA, Lisbon

substantially increase the risk of a fatal overdose. Acute deaths relating solely to cocaine or amphetamine intoxication are unusual, and deaths related to ecstasy or similar substances, although widely publicised, are actually few in number. This might change, however, if chronic intense use develops, or if the use of these drugs in combination with other substances increases.

How many drug addicts are there in the EU?

There are no accurate statistics on the number of drug addicts in the EU because drug use is largely hidden. Instead, the figure can only be estimated using various statistical techniques. The end result is usually presented as a 'probable range' and should therefore be interpreted with caution. At present, most estimates for individual EU countries are between two and ten addicts per 1,000 population aged 15-54. The total number of heroin addicts in the EU is estimated to be about 1 million. If use of other drugs such as amphetamines and cocaine were included, and the definition broadened to include those who are not strictly dependent (addicted) but who regularly use illegal drugs in sufficient amounts to be at high risk of experiencing serious problems, then the number would be considerably higher.

Is AIDS still a problem among drug users?

AIDS statistics among injecting drug users are declining as a result of behavioural changes and improved treatment of the disease. However, as current AIDS sufferers tend to have been infected on average ten years ago, this gives little information about the current rate of infection. There are indications that, although infection rates are lower than in the 1980s, new infections do still occur, particularly in young and new injecting drug users. Prevalence rates of other infections, such as hepatitis C, are extremely high – mostly over 50% and up to 92% – which also indicates that risk behaviour continues. In an attempt to combat this problem, more and more EU countries are adopting prevention measures such as syringe-exchange programmes.

■ The above information is from the European Monitoring Centre for Drugs and Drug Addiction's (EMCDDA) web site which can be found at www.emcdda.org

© European Monitoring Centre for Drugs and Drug Addiction (EMCDDA)

Young cannabis users at more risk of mental illness

By David Derbyshire, Science Correspondent

Teenagers who smoke cannabis are risking depression and schizophrenia later in life, three new studies conclude today.

Researchers have found that adolescents who use the drug at least once a week are increasing the chances of suffering serious mental illness. Girls are particularly at risk. One study found that smoking the drug each day increases the risk of depression five times; weekly use doubles the risk.

The links between cannabis and mental health have been debated for decades. But the new research, published today in the *British Medical Journal*, highlights the dangers to adolescents.

A study of 1,600 students in Australia between 1992 and 1998 found that frequent use of the drug led to depression and anxiety, particularly in girls. Around 60 per cent had used cannabis by the age of 20, and seven per cent said that they were daily users.

After taking into account other lifestyle factors, the researchers found that daily use increased the risk of depression fivefold in girls in young adulthood, while weekly use doubled the risk.

The research was led by Prof George Patton of the Murdoch Children's Research Institute, Parkville, Victoria. Prof Patton said: 'Strategies to reduce frequent use of cannabis might reduce the level of mental disorders in young people.'

The other two studies looked at the links between cannabis and schizophrenia. One, led by Dr Stanley Zammit, of the University of Wales, Cardiff, found that cannabis increased the risk of schizophrenia by 30 per cent.

The study was of 50,000 Swedish conscripts carried out over 27 years. Self-medication with cannabis was an 'unlikely explanation' for the link, they found.

The third study found that the earlier teenagers start using cannabis, the greater the risk of schizophrenia. Those aged 15 in the study, led by researchers at King's College London, were four times more likely to have schizophrenia aged 26 than teenagers who did not use the drug.

One in ten of the people who used cannabis by the age of 15 in the sample developed schizophrenia by the time they were 26, compared with three per cent of later users and non-users, they found.

Marjorie Wallace, chief executive of the mental health charity Sane, said: 'While cannabis may be harmless to many people, there is no way of telling who might be the vulnerable victim for whom its use can turn from a relaxing trip into a lifelong torment.'

© *Telegraph Group Limited, London 2003*

Zero tolerance conceals drug use in schools

Schools' zero tolerance policies towards drugs may be counter-productive because they encourage children to conceal drug problems, according to Home Office research.

Experts who studied the drug habits of 300 hardcore young offenders concluded that low or zero tolerance policies 'may not be helpful'.

The research was published as the drugs minister, Bob Ainsworth, unveiled a new £40m programme of drug treatment services for young offenders.

Mr Ainsworth also announced £30m for drug work in young offenders' institutes' secure units, £22m for councils to provide specialist youth workers, and £15m for schemes that use sport to steer young people away from drugs.

He said: 'Vulnerable young people need prevention and treatment before the problems escalate.'

The Home Office report said that zero tolerance policies encouraged 'children to conceal rather than deal with their drug use'.

It warned that those pupils excluded from school as a result of using drugs were not necessarily the only or the worst offenders.

The study's conclusions contrast sharply with guidance from the Department for Education and Skills, which has increased headteachers' powers to expel drug-dealing pupils.

The charity DrugScope said the research showed that zero tolerance drug policies led to drug problems being ignored rather than dealt with effectively.

The Home Office report said that zero tolerance policies encouraged 'children to conceal rather than deal with their drug use'

Helen Wilkinson, director of information and policy at the charity, said: 'Research shows drug use among excluded children is much higher than for those in school.

'A range of disciplinary and supportive measures is necessary. We should be helping children with problems. Throwing them out simply exacerbates the problem.'

But the general secretary of the Secondary Heads' Association, Dr John Dunford, said: 'We would reject

any notion that drug people should not be excluded from school.

'I think schools can safely ignore the views of this Home Office research.

'Selling drugs is a crime outside school and it has to be dealt with severely inside school as well.'

Last May the DfES said children caught dealing drugs at schools should be expelled with no chance of a reprieve, even for a first-time offence.

A fifth of the group studied for the Home Office report had dealt drugs, shoplifted, sold stolen goods or gone joyriding at least 20 times in the previous year.

More than 85% had used cannabis, alcohol and tobacco but heroin and crack cocaine use were still comparatively low.

'There was no evidence of a progression towards heroin or crack cocaine use or dependence despite the diverse drug use amongst the group,' said the report.

The 293 young people surveyed by researchers from Essex University were all being supervised by youth offending teams – 52% were 15 or 16 years old while a handful were under 14.

The Home Office today also published reports showing 42% of young homeless people had taken heroin and 38% crack cocaine – about 20 times the average.

Young people who had been in care also reported higher than average drug use, with 10% using crack or heroin.

Tackling young people's drug problems

£107 million to tackle young people's drug problems

A £107 million package of measures to help steer vulnerable young people away from a life of drugs and crime was announced today by Home Office Minister, Bob Ainsworth.

For the first time treatment and drug services will be targeted at under-18s who are starting to use Class A drugs and turning to crime to fund their habit and a new Youth Crime Programme will work directly with young drug users in communities particularly affected by drug-related crime.

The new package, designed to help young offenders break the link between drugs and crime, will include over the next three years:

- £22 million for local authorities to provide specialist workers and training services for young people at risk;
- £15 million to fund 50 new Positive Futures projects – schemes to steer young people away from drug misuse through sport;
- £30 million will provide prevention, treatment and follow-up care in all juvenile custodial institutions. We aim to have drug workers in all custodial institutions by December 2003; and
- £40 million to pilot and roll out Youth Crime Programmes to areas particularly affected by drug-related crime. The programme will include treatment and services and will target under-18s at each stage of the youth justice system.

Announcing the new measures, Mr Ainsworth said:

'Getting and keeping young people away from drugs is the highest priority in the Government's Drug Strategy. Vulnerable young people need prevention and treatment before the problems escalate. Often these young people do not just have

drug problems, they have a range of problems, which all need to be tackled by local agencies working closely together.

'We are already helping 16,000 vulnerable young people to deal with drug-related problems and by 2006 we will be capable of helping 50,000. It is vital that this help is effective and makes measurable improvements in reducing drug crime as well as improving education, employment and health.

'The funding and programmes we have announced today will make a real difference to the lives of vulnerable young people and help local agencies to work fully together. By targeting young people we plan to prevent another generation of drug addicts and offenders, tackle drug-related crime and help communities

---

'We are already helping 16,000 vulnerable young people to deal with drug-related problems and by 2006 we will be capable of helping 50,000'

---

to get rid of the scourge that drugs can cause.'

The new Youth Crime Programme will target young offenders and will pilot measures such as drug testing and treatment referral aimed specifically at young people to help break the link between drugs and crime. The Programme will be piloted in some of the 30 areas, announced on 21 January, which are particularly affected by drug-related crime. The Programme will use new powers proposed in the Criminal Justice and Sentencing Bill to test 14-17-year-old offenders for heroin and crack/cocaine.

The Home Office also today published three reports which provide those working with young people with more information about drug use by young offenders, young homeless people and young people looked after by social services. We have also jointly published with DrugScope new guidance for Drug Action Teams on how to identify and treat young people with substance misuse problems.

- The above information is from the Government web site www.drugs.gov.uk

Drug proofing your kids

Information from Care for the Family

Is it possible to drug proof our kids? If we mean, can parents stop them from trying cigarettes, alcohol and illicit drugs, the answer is 'No!' But if we mean, can parents influence their choices positively in relation to drug use, the answer is a definite 'Yes!' Paul Carter spoke to Wendy Bray.

Risk-taking is a normal part of adolescence, as is stretching and testing parental boundaries. But faced with the threat of drugs, parents often don't know how to respond. It may be easier to deny the risk and say, 'It won't happen to my kids.'

Paul Carter works at the YMCA in Plymouth. He is actively involved in youth work, youth leader training and workshops with parents, and is seconded one day a week to the national drug education charity, Hope UK. Plymouth may be a seaside city in sleepy Devon but, like every city, it struggles with a significant drug problem. I suggested to Paul that it's easy for drug and alcohol abuse to be pushed 'out of sight and out of mind' by the majority of people.

Risk-taking is a normal part of adolescence, as is stretching and testing parental boundaries

---

'We can certainly adopt a mentality of "it doesn't happen here", agreed Paul. 'It's often the result of fear, rather than ignorance. Yet we only have to look at our local paper to find that hardly a day goes by without a drug and alcohol abuse related story being featured. And research tells us that 50% of British children will take drugs at some point – that's more than any other European country.'

No immunity

'No child is immune. Every school will face drug and alcohol problems and every teenager will know someone,

who knows someone, who can get hold of drugs. Churches are certainly not immune – and many now recognise that drug and alcohol issues must be on their agenda. Not just for those on "the fringe", but to educate and support their own young people and, perhaps more importantly, parents.'

Parents are often scared, not just of the consequences of drugs and alcohol, but the fact that their kids know more about them than they do. 'We want to feel "in control", but actually we're out of our depth,' I suggested.

'That's exactly why parents should make sure they are educated in drugs issues, and can understand what their kids are talking about,' explained Paul. 'Then they can listen and talk to them in an informed way and develop an action plan for prevention, by offering a positive, alternative lifestyle.'

Awareness and education are a big priority for Paul – both in the local community, with parents, and in schools. He sees programmes like Care for the Family's 'How to Drug Proof Your Kids' and Hope UK's 'Drugnet' and 'Childwise' as essential if the tide is to be turned. He believes our young people need to know that we are ,okay to talk about drugs' and send messages that we understand the pressures they face and that we are on their side.

Identity

Young people struggle with finding their own identity and their self-esteem can be in their boots. They need to know that life can be lived to the full – without the use of drugs and alcohol.

'They look for our support as they make choices which are much harder than any we had to make as teenagers. It's harder to speak against the crowd and walk away from what you know is wrong or harmful,' said Paul.

■ The above information is from *Care for the Family* magazine, January 2003, produced by Care for the Family. See page 41 for their address details.

© *Care for the Family*

Drugs: what you should know

Information from KidsHealth.org

These days, drugs can be found everywhere, and it may seem like everyone's doing them. Many teens are tempted by the excitement or escape that drugs seem to offer. But learning the facts about drugs can help you see them for what they are – and can help you steer clear. Read on to learn more.

The skinny on substances

Thanks to medical and drug research, there are thousands of drugs that help people. Antibiotics and vaccines have revolutionised the treatment of infections. There are medicines to lower blood pressure, treat diabetes, and reduce the body's rejection of new organs. Medicines can cure, slow, or prevent disease, helping us to lead healthier and happier lives. But there are also lots of illegal, harmful drugs that people take to help them feel good or have a good time.

How do drugs work? Drugs are chemicals or substances that change the way our bodies work. When you put them into your body (often by swallowing, inhaling, or injecting them), drugs find their way into your bloodstream and are transported to parts of your body, such as your brain. In the brain, drugs may either intensify or dull your senses, alter your sense of alertness, and sometimes decrease physical pain. A drug may be helpful or harmful. The effects of drugs can vary depending upon the kind of drug taken, how much is

> *Some teens believe drugs will help them think better, be more popular, stay more active, or become a better athlete*

taken, how often it is used, how quickly it gets to the brain, and what other drugs, food, or substances are taken at the same time.

Many substances can harm your body and your brain. Drinking alcohol, smoking tobacco, taking illegal drugs, and sniffing glue can all cause serious damage to the human body. Some drugs severely impair a person's ability to make healthy choices and decisions. Teens who drink, for example, are more likely to get involved in dangerous situations, such as driving under the influence or having unprotected sex.

And just as there are many kinds of drugs available, there are as many reasons for trying drugs or starting to use drugs regularly. Some teens take drugs just for the pleasure they believe they can bring. Many times, someone tried to convince them that drugs would make them feel good or that they'd have a better time if they took them.

Some teens believe drugs will help them think better, be more popular, stay more active, or become a better athlete. Others are simply curious and figure one try won't hurt. Others want to fit in. Many teens use drugs to gain attention from their parents or because they are depressed or think drugs will help them escape their problems. The truth is, drugs don't solve problems. Drugs simply hide feelings and problems. When a drug wears off, the feelings and problems remain – or become worse. Drugs can ruin every aspect of a person's life.

> *The truth is, drugs don't solve problems. Drugs simply hide feelings and problems. When a drug wears off, the feelings and problems remain – or become worse.*

■ This information was provided by KidsHealth, one of the largest resources online for medically reviewed health information written for parents, kids, and teens. For more articles like this one, visit www.KidsHealth.org or www.TeensHealth.org

© *KidsHealth.org*

Risk reduction

Information from the Libra Project

This information has been produced to help those people who use any substance to do so more safely (by 'substance' we mean any drug, legal (like alcohol) or illegal (like E), prescribed or not). Any substance use carries risk; by establishing what risks you are engaging in (through self-assessment) and finding areas where risk can be reduced, you can minimise the likelihood of harm. The only way to ensure that you engage in no risk at all is of course not to use any substance. If you are not currently using any substance, these pages hold valuable information that you may be able to pass on to friends who do.

What are the risks?

The idea that the main risk involved in substance use is a 'long slippery slope' inevitably leading to addiction and death is mistaken and misleading. This fear can obscure many of the real risks involved when we use substances. Cannabis by itself does not kill people, but this does not mean that using it is a risk-free activity. Risks might be physical, psychological, short-term or long-term (or a combination of all of these). Risks may relate to the substance itself, or how, where and why it is being used. Risks are clearly increased when a variety of substances are being used together, or when a substance is used regularly over a prolonged period of time. Safer substance use starts with assessing the risks you are engaging in.

Risk assessment

How much do you know about the substance (or substances) you are using? One of the most obvious risks is using a substance you know nothing about. Information about risks relating to specific substances is available from a variety of sources (more on this later). Even if you know the specific risks for the substance you are using, this information will not help you unless you act on it, or if the substance you have acquired is not what you think it is (a particular risk when taking illegally-sold pills, capsules and powders). How you get the substance into your body dramatically affects the risks you engage in. The method that carries the most risk of harm is injection. Injecting might be seen as a cost-effective way of taking a substance, but this is a false economy. There are a whole range of issues that are presented to any person who uses a substance in this way. There are a range of viruses (including HIV and hepatitis) that are carried in the body fluids of infected people (who may themselves appear perfectly

healthy). These viruses can be passed on if you share any injecting equipment (including water, filters, citric/lemon juice, spoons, needles and barrels). Infections can also come from dirty (i.e. non-sterile) equipment, and unsafe injecting practices. Pills and powders that have been produced in illicit laboratories (like E, speed, heroin and cocaine) won't be sterile, and will contain adulterants – other substances that add bulk to what you buy. Sometimes the adulterants will be toxic, and this can lead to damage. Generally, the least risk will come from swallowing a substance – our bodies are able to recognise a range of toxins which can be filtered by the gut (or expelled). Sniffing (or snorting) powders can lead to immediate damage, especially if the powder is severely adulterated (for example with a cleaning agent like Vim or Harpic). Regularly smoking any substance is likely to lead to respiratory problems. Once a powder has been cut (or adulterated) there is no indication of how concentrated it is. Recent confiscations of street 'speed' have contained as little as 4% of amphetamine sulphate in the powder. Occasionally a powder with an unusually high purity (maybe as high as 80%) will be sold, usually by

Risks might be physical, psychological, short-term or long-term (or a combination of all of these)

an inexperienced dealer. This may sound like a bonus, but taking a substance that is so pure is likely to lead to an overdose – effectively you could be doubling or even tripling the quantity you would normally use. We take drugs to affect how we feel, our behaviour and our perception of the world. Some risks come from these changes – our behaviour may become less inhibited; we may be more likely to engage in unsafe sex, react violently to situations or make decisions which we later regret. All substance use changes our perception to some extent. This can affect our ability to react quickly – for example when driving or cycling – or can make a 'normal' activity more dangerous (like crossing roads, swimming, dancing and climbing stairs). There is a big difference between taking a drug to change how you feel and taking a drug to enhance how you feel. If you use a substance to lift you out of a depression or relieve yourself from stress, the result will only ever be short term. Drugs don't take problems away. They can mask problems, or make them seem less important, but they don't resolve them. The danger is that someone who uses a substance to deal with an unchanging situation has to continually use the substance. Most substances (especially hallucinogens) enhance and amplify our feelings – taking LSD when you're in a bad mood is unlikely to result in a 'good' experience. A good way to assess your own substance use is to ask yourself a few questions . . . How much do you really know about the substance you are using? Do you use every day? Do you mix with people who don't use? Can you afford your substance use? Do you have good times without using drugs? Does your substance use adversely affect other aspects of your life (like employment, studies or relationships)? Any patterns or aspects of your use that concern you can be checked out with others.

We take drugs
to affect how we feel,
our behaviour and our
perception of the world

The danger is
that someone who uses a
substance to deal with an
unchanging situation has
to continually use
the substance

Risk reduction

So, you've explored your substance use, become aware of the risks you are engaging in – now what? Reducing risks is not difficult. When you are planning to use a substance, think ahead and make the experience as safe as you can. Seek information about the substance; if you are buying it illegally then be aware that the substance has not been through any 'quality control' – if you've decided to buy, then buy from someone you trust rather than a complete stranger. If you are injecting, use sterile equipment (available from needle exchanges). Think (honestly) about how you feel – are you taking the substance to have a 'good' time or to escape a 'bad' time? Plan ahead – make sure that you are as unlikely as possible to encounter a stressful or dangerous environment. Will you feel safe? Will you feel comfortable (or threatened)? Will someone you know be there to look after you if you do get into difficulty? It's far better to think all of this through before you take a substance rather than panicking whilst you're using.

Legal issues

Up until now, we've avoided mentioning what can be some people's main fear – the law. There is nothing more likely to bring you down with a crash than being busted. If you are taking illegal drugs, find out about the legal issues involved and your rights. If you are searched, questioned or arrested by the police and are not sure of your rights, the charity RELEASE are available 24 hours a day to advise you. Their helpline number is (020) 7729 9904, and you can ask the Desk Sergeant to contact them for you if you are taken to a Police Station. It is wise to exercise your right to silence until you have spoken to them or a solicitor.

■ The above information is from the Libra Project's web site: www.brookes.ac.uk/health/libra/index.html © *Libra Project*

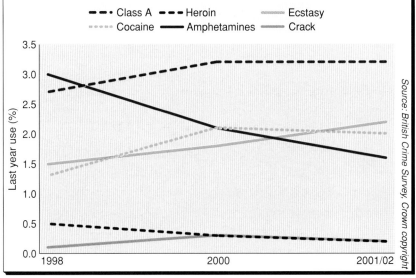

Patterns of drug use among 16- to 59-year-olds

Comparing last year prevalence estimates for 16- to 59-year-olds from the 2000 *British Crime Survey* with those from the 2001/2002 sweep, there have been statistically significant decreases in the use of amphetamines, crack, heroin, LSD, magic mushrooms and steroids. However, over the same period there were statistically significant increases in the use of ecstasy. The graphic below shows the change from 1998 to 2001/2002 in the last year prevalence for Class A and the main drugs for 16- to 59-year-olds.

Last year use of drugs among 16- to 59-year-olds

Legend: Class A, Heroin, Ecstasy, Cocaine, Amphetamines, Crack

Source: British Crime Survey, Crown copyright

New drugs strategy

New drugs strategy is a step in the right direction – now let's get running, says Turning Point

Social care charity Turning Point today welcomed the Government's revised drugs strategy as a step in the right direction, but reminded ministers of the challenge ahead in tackling the reality of drug misuse problems in the UK.

Chief Executive Lord Victor Adebowale said: 'These are welcome steps in the right direction, but the challenge is to start running, and running fast enough to tackle the reality of drug misuse problems in the UK.

'As a social care organisation, Turning Point knows that treatment works when it meets the complex needs of drug users. Treatment must reflect the wider social context of drug misuse, so the strategy's emphasis on more specific interventions, support for families and carers and more routes into treatment are all good news.

'But in many ways this strategy does not go far enough. We see the beginnings of a rational approach but these words must translate into action and deliver real improvements to services on the ground. Treatment is all too often characterised by poor availability in parts of the country, lengthy delays and weak assessments that don't meet people's needs.

'We need more action to give former drug users better after-care – making sure they have ongoing help to stay off drugs.

'We need more action to make harm minimisation a reality – the Government should make working with current drug users easier not harder.

> *The challenge is to start running, and running fast enough to tackle the reality of drug misuse problems in the UK*

'And we need action to tackle the shortfall of services, particularly those geared towards people with mental health problems and people from minority ethnic communities.

'Another issue is the lack of recognition of alcohol as a drug. Almost twice as many people are dependent on alcohol as on all other drugs and we need to develop services that treat all aspects of substance misuse.'

The Government's revised drugs strategy was launched after a visit by Home Secretary David Blunkett to Turning Point's flagship Hungerford service, a street agency which offers advice, support, information and treatment to vulnerable and hard-to-reach groups, their families and friends.

■ The above information is from Turning Point's web site which can be found at www.turning-point.co.uk

© Turning Point

Tackling the drugs problem

David Blunkett publishes updated drug strategy: 'Educate, Prevent and Treat – Key to Success in Tackling Drugs Problem'

All controlled drugs are harmful and will remain illegal, the Home Secretary David Blunkett reaffirmed today as he published an updated drug strategy focusing on delivery and evidence of what works on the ground.

Educating young people about the dangers of drugs, preventing drug misuse, combating the dealers and treating addicts are the key elements of the strategy. A major increase in direct annual funding will underpin the Government's commitment to tackle drugs and the harm they cause. Funding will increase from a planned £1.026 billion in this financial year, to £1.244 billion in the next financial year, rising to a total annual spend of nearly £1.5 billion in the year starting April 2005.

A significant proportion of the funding will be targeted on getting drug-using offenders into treatment. Every opportunity from arrest, to court, to sentence, to parole will be used to get offenders into treatment and out of trouble.

Starting from next year in the highest crime areas with the worst drugs problems the Government will roll out a comprehensive end-to-end approach. This will ensure that every drug-addicted offender is identified through drug testing at the point of arrest and charge and given the choice at their bail hearing of entering treatment rather than entering custody. All this will be backed up by extra resources for arrest referral, drug treatment and testing orders, treatment in prison and YOIs and for post-release treatment and support for those leaving custody.

As well as the impact on crime, drug misuse has dire consequences for the health of individuals, their families and society as a whole. That is why the Secretary of State for Health established the National Treatment Agency (NTA) last year to increase the provision and quality of drug treatment. The NTA is concentrating on ensuring that appropriate treatment is available for everyone who needs it and that waiting times for treatment are reduced.

The updated strategy, promised when the Home Secretary delivered his response to the Home Affairs Select Committee in July, is based on what works best to deal with drug problems. It includes:

- A tougher focus on Class A drugs.
- New cross-regional police 'hit squads' to break up middle drug markets, the link in the chain between traffickers and local dealers.
- A stronger focus on the 250,000 Class A drug users with the most severe problems who account for 99% of the costs of drug abuse.
- Better targeting, focusing on the communities with the greatest need.
- Expansion of treatment services tailored to individual need, including residential treatment where appropriate and reduced waiting times.

'Young people are our highest priority. They need good quality drug education, information and advice based on a credible assessment of the damage drugs do'

- New improved treatment for crack and cocaine users, heroin prescribing for all those who would benefit from it and more harm minimisation – with improved access to GP medical services. Funding for treatment services, including prisons, will increase by £45 million in the next financial year, £54 million for the year starting from April 2004 and £115 million from April 2005. This will be boosted by treatment funding associated with Drug Treatment and Testing Orders of nearly £10 million in the next financial year, £12

million in the year starting from April 2004 and £16 million from April £2005 – bringing the total direct annual spend on treatment up to £589 million by 2005.

- An innovative advertising campaign, to be launched in the spring to educate the young about the dangers of drugs and prevent them from falling into drug misuse.
- More support for parents, carers and families so they can easily access advice, help, counselling and mutual support, expanded outreach and community treatment for vulnerable young people.
- Improved services in those communities affected by crack, fast-track crack treatment programmes in the worst affected areas and new police initiatives to close crack markets.
- New aftercare and throughcare services to improve community access to treatment and ensure that people leaving prison and treatment avoid the revolving door back into addiction and offending.

The Home Office will be working with the Strategy Unit at Number 10 to review the impact of enforcement work on the drug supply chain from international production to distribution in the UK so that work can be focused where it will do the most damage to drug dealers.

Announcing the updated strategy David Blunkett said: 'All controlled drugs are harmful and will remain illegal. The misery caused by the use of drugs and hard drugs that kill cannot be underestimated. It damages the health and life chances of individuals; it undermines family life, tears apart communities and turns law-abiding citizens into thieves. We will maintain our focus on Class A drugs as they cause the most harm. We must achieve real reductions in the level of problematic use if we are to turn around the lives of individuals and their communities.

'This updated drug strategy is a chance to build on what we have learnt. Education, prevention, minimising harm, treatment and effective policing are our most powerful tools in dealing with drugs.

'The best place for drug using offenders is in treatment and out of trouble. Presumption against bail is tough love – accept the treatment on offer or face custody

---

'Young people are our highest priority. They need good quality drug education, information and advice based on a credible assessment of the damage drugs do.

'The best place for drug using offenders is in treatment and out of trouble. Presumption against bail is tough love – accept the treatment on offer or face custody.

'We are not starting from scratch. We are learning from, building on, and adapting the 10-year strategy adopted in 1998. If we are to succeed, we must have continuity, persistence and the determination to make a real difference. Future generations should never have to face the dangers and harm that drugs present to too many of our young people, their families and their communities today.'

Health Secretary Alan Milburn said: 'I welcome this opportunity to build on the success of the 1998 Drug Strategy. The revised strategy shows that we are currently on track to meet our target of increasing the number of drug misusers in treatment through developing better quality treatment programmes and more of them. Reducing drug use is a key

Government priority and my department remains committed to ensuring that the significant funds being allocated are targeted at the areas where the need is greatest.'

The new drug strategy updates the 1998 strategy and is being published alongside research about levels and costs of drug use.

Key features of the updated drug strategy:

- A tougher focus on Class A drugs. The misery caused by the use of crack, cocaine, heroin and ecstasy cannot be underestimated.
- A stronger focus on education, prevention, enforcement and treatment to prevent and tackle problematic drug use. The 250,000 Class A drug users with the most severe problems who account for 99% of the costs of drug abuse in England and Wales and do most harm to themselves, their families and communities.
- More resources. Planned direct annual expenditure for tackling drugs will rise from £1.026 billion in this financial year to £1.244 billion in the next financial year, £1.344 billion in the year starting April 2004 to a total annual spend of nearly £1.5 billion in the year starting April 2005 – an increase of 44%.

New areas of spend include:

- More support for parents, carers and families so they can easily access advice, help, counselling and mutual support, a new education campaign for young people based on credible information of the harm which drugs cause, increased outreach and community treatment for vulnerable young people and expanded testing and referrals into treatment within the youth justice system so that by 2006 we will be able to provide support to 40-50,000 vulnerable young people a year.
- Reducing the availability of drugs on the streets through new cross-regional teams to tackle 'middle markets' – the link in the chain from traffickers to local dealers, targeted policing to crack down on crack, and increased assistance to the Afghan Government to achieve their aim of reducing

---

Future generations should never have to face the dangers and harm that drugs present to too many of our young people

---

opium production with a view to eliminating it by 2013. A review of the impact of interventions on the drug supply chain from international production to distribution within the UK by the Government's Strategy Unit working with the Home Office and other key departments.

- Further expansion of treatment services appropriate for individual need, reduced waiting times, improved treatment for crack and cocaine, heroin prescribing for all those who would benefit from it and more harm minimisation – with improved access to GP medical services. By 2008, we will have the capacity to treat 200,000 problematic drug users.
- A major expansion of services within the criminal justice system using every opportunity from arrest, to court, to sentence, to get drug misusing offenders into treatment – including expanded testing, improved referrals, and new and expanded community sentences. By March 2005, we will have doubled the number of Drug Treatment and Testing Orders.
- New aftercare and throughcare services to improve community access to treatment and ensure those leaving prison and treatment avoid the revolving door back into addiction and offending. By April 2005, all drug action teams will have a co-ordinated system of aftercare in place.
- Better targeting: focusing on the communities with the greatest need.
- We will be strengthening capacity to deliver in those areas which have the greatest problems. Although services will be rolled out across the country we will be piloting and developing new

services for young people and new interventions within the criminal justice system, first in the areas of greatest need.

- We will improve services in those communities affected by crack. The action plan on crack will lead to fast-track crack treatment programmes in the worst affected areas, new police initiatives to close crack markets and new diversionary programmes for young people.
- A renewed emphasis on delivery and revised targets which are challenging but achievable: reducing the use of the most dangerous drugs and patterns of drug use by young people, with a particular focus on the most vulnerable; tackling prevalence through a three-pronged attack on supply, dealers and traffickers, and assets, and on working with the Afghan Government to reduce opium supply; reducing drug-related crime; and continuing to expand drug treatment but also improving its quality.

- The above information is from the Government web site www.drugs.gov.uk

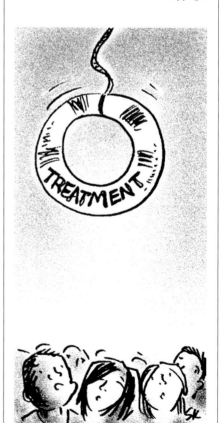

Getting into trouble with drugs

At college

Unfortunately even today, some colleges and universities take alarmist approaches to drug use and will do all in their powers to be seen 'stamping out' drug use. This often means dismissing those students found or suspected of using drugs.

Each college has its own policies and practices so we are unable to give you comprehensive guidelines on what to expect. Some staff in student services may be better than others so it's best to check with the students' union first before seeking help for yourself or a friend through the college.

Having drugs for your own use is one thing, but supplying drugs to others is quite another. The law doesn't differentiate between buying a little extra to sell on to a few friends and dealing more widely. Colleges and universities will also take any dealing seriously, many will take punitive action even where very small amounts of a drug are involved. One course of action is to refuse student accommodation to those suspected or found dealing, growing or producing on the premises. Carrying out any of these activities in your student flat has consequences not only for yourself, but also on

By Gary Hayes

your flat mates and the college renting out the flat. Be aware that some colleges will always involve the police if they believe criminal activity is taking place either in your student flat or on campus.

The police and the law
Caution

This is a complex area where we can only provide general guidelines. Anyone in difficulties with the law should get legal advice at the earliest opportunity by contacting their solicitor or Release on 020 7729 9904 (24 hours).

The Misuse of Drugs Act

The main law controlling the use of drugs is the Misuse of Drugs Act. It divides drugs into three classes A-C. Class A drugs are regarded as the most dangerous and so carry the heaviest penalties.

The drugs
Class A drugs

Cocaine and crack, ecstasy, heroin, methadone, processed magic mushrooms, LSD.

Class B drugs

Amphetamine, cannabis resin and herb, codeine and some other strong painkillers.

Class C drugs

Steroids and tranquillisers (supply is the main offence here).

Magic Mushrooms

It is not an offence to possess magic mushrooms in their natural state. However, psilocin and psilocybin, the drugs that they contain, are Class A drugs. So if the mushrooms are intentionally prepared by, for example, drying, freezing or pickling, then you might be charged with possession, supply, intent to supply or even production.

The main offences

The most common offence is possession of a controlled drug. This includes joint possession of a common pool of drugs and past possession, when past drug use is admitted. There is no offence if you are found with a drug you didn't know was there (e.g. if a friend put it in your pocket) but you might have to prove this in court. More serious offences are supply and intention to supply. Remember, supply includes giving or selling drugs to a friend, or even looking after them for someone else. People who say, 'the drugs were not all for me, some were for a friend' usually make things worse for themselves by admitting supply. The heaviest penalties under the law concern the import and supply of controlled drugs.

Making or growing your own

Cultivation of cannabis is also an offence. Penalties are more severe if the court believes cultivation was intended to supply others. It is not an offence to possess cannabis seeds.

Manufacturing illegal drugs will be dealt with severely, usually in excess of what is given out for supply. Some drugs which are not illegal to possess such as Ketamine, GHB, herbal ecstasy, or poppers are covered by the Medicines Act 1968 which means that it is illegal to manufacture or sell such drugs without proper authorisation.

Prosecution and punishment

There are numerous factors to take into account in determining the likely punishment for any particular offence. Different police forces have their own approach to drug offences. Whilst some will caution for first-time offenders, others will always prosecute. There are also variations depending on whether the case is tried by a Magistrates' Court or a Crown Court, who deal out the heavier punishments. The maximum penalties can be summarised as follows:

Possession	Supply
Class A drug	
7 years + fine	Life + fine
Class B drug	
5 years + fine	14 years + fine
Class C drug	
2 years + fine	5 years + fine

In reality maximum sentences are rarely imposed, usually only for repeat offenders involved in serious offences. Many aggravating and mitigating factors can operate, such as the amount of the drug involved, whether it was a first offence or not and the defendant's character. As a general rule for supply-type offences you will normally be sent to prison. For a simple possession offence you will tend to get a non-custodial sentence.

Drugs and driving

Under the Road Traffic Act 1988 it is an offence to drive or be in charge of a motor vehicle when unfit through drugs. If guilty of driving when unfit, there's an obligatory 12 months' disqualification and a fine; often longer periods are imposed. In cases involving accidents or other aggravating circumstances, then longer disqualifications, stiffer fines and imprisonment can apply. It is also an offence to be drunk whilst in charge of a vehicle (even just sleeping it off in your car!).

Your rights

You can be stopped and searched if the police have reasonable suspicion that you are in possession of a controlled drug. They cannot carry out an intimate search or remove hats or outer clothing in public view.

Remember: in a police station you have the right to be treated humanely and with respect; to know why you have been arrested; to speak to the custody officer; to have someone notified of your arrest; to consult with your own solicitor or the Duty solicitor privately; to speak to Release who will put you in contact with a lawyer. These rights can sometimes be delayed, but no one can refuse them.

Employment

Having a record

If you have been prosecuted for any offence, this will be stored on a police database, referred to as your criminal record. Having a record, and in particular for something drug related, will put off many employers.

Many professions automatically exclude individuals with past convictions related to drugs, these include in particular the judicial, medical sectors, and professions working with children. If you don't reveal your record and the employer finds out later, you will almost certainly be sacked. After a period of time, some convictions are 'spent' and do not have to be disclosed. Some jobs are exempt from this. Getting caught therefore with an illegal drug on you can damage many study and career ambitions. So bear this in mind if you come in contact with drugs.

Drug testing

If you are going for a job interview, you may face a drug test, even if the job has nothing to do with public safety. The police and armed services usually drug test new recruits, as well as some commercial companies. Most

---

Getting caught with an illegal drug on you can damage many study and career ambitions

---

tests involve taking a sample of urine. Drugs will stay in the system for some time after you have taken them. How long that will be is different for every drug and will also depend on many other factors like individual metabolism. So what follows is only a very rough guide.

Drug	*Detection periods in urine*
Alcohol	12-24 hours
Amphetamine	2-4 days
Cannabis	30 days for heavy use
Cocaine/crack	12 hrs – 3 days
Dia-/Temazepam	1-2 days
Ecstasy	2-4 days
Heroin	1-2 days
LSD	2-3 days
Methadone	2 days

Traces of drug use can also be found on body hair: the longer the hair, the more drug history can be revealed. This method of testing is proving increasingly popular with, for example, the police.

Drugs and travelling abroad

If you are travelling abroad it is important to know the laws regarding drugs in the different countries you may visit as well as the laws in the UK on your return. A common misconception is that drugs bought legally in one country can be carried to another country. Cannabis or mushrooms bought in Holland, for example, cannot be brought into other European countries. If you have some drugs left after a visit, do not try to take them out with you for the sake of a few guilders or pesetas – get rid of them. Scandinavian countries in particular have greater restrictions on imports and exclude some medicines and herbal remedies such as Khat and even codeine. Outside Europe a number of countries do not take kindly to people bringing in illegal substances and threaten the death penalty to those found guilty of drug trafficking. Therefore, before you set off, find out what medication or other drugs you can and can't take with you. The national embassies in London are a good source of information.

■ The above information is from DrugScope's web site which can be found at www.drugscope.org.uk

© *DrugScope*

Britain's drug habit

Exclusive poll shows more than half of young flout law

More than half of Britain's 16- to 24-year-olds have taken illegal drugs, according to one of the most extensive studies undertaken into the growing drug culture.

The news comes as the Government prepares a significant relaxation of drugs laws, the *Observer* can reveal.

More people now believe tobacco is a 'drug of greater risk' than ecstasy, according to the *Observer/ICM* poll, which also reveals that more than 5 million people regularly use cannabis, 2.4m ecstasy and 2m amphetamines and cocaine.

Two in five people between 25 and 34 and more than a third of 35- to 44-year-olds say they have taken unlawful drugs, confirming that drug use is more prevalent than previously believed. The findings, in a poll commissioned as part of a months-long investigation into drug use published today in *Drugs Uncovered*, a special 64-page magazine free with the *Observer*, will increase pressure on the Home Office to speed up reform of drugs laws.

David Blunkett, the Home Secretary, is now set to lay fresh legislation before Parliament in June to allow the reclassification of cannabis from Class B to Class C, a move which many see in effect as decriminalisation.

Government officials said that two of Blunkett's three 'tests' on cannabis had now been met. Firstly, the Advisory Council on the Misuse of Drugs reported earlier this year that it supported reclassification of cannabis. Secondly, in Lambeth, London, an experiment by the Metropolitan Police under which users have .cannabis seized rather than face arrest has been seen as a success, with wide public support.

The third test is the long-awaited Home Affairs Select Committee report on drugs which, as the *Observer* revealed earlier in the year, will also back the move when it is

By Ben Summerskill and Kamal Ahmed

published in mid-May. Sources said Blunkett would then 'lay an order in council', allowing an amendment to the Misuse of Drugs Act.

In another signal that Blunkett is softening his line on drugs, in December GPs will be sent new guidelines on prescribing heroin. Published by the Department of Health under pressure from the Home Office, these will say that doctors should be more willing to prescribe the drug to addicts. The Home Office hopes that up to 1,500 heroin addicts could be helped. At the moment only 300 are prescribed heroin by GPs, a tiny percentage of the 270,000 heroin addicts in the country.

The *Observer* poll reveals that 28 per cent of people over 16-13 million adults – have taken illegal drugs. Men are twice as likely to have taken drugs as women. Two million people say they took drugs while under 14. Four out of five illegal drug users have taken cannabis, 27 per cent ecstasy, 25 per cent amphetamines and more than one in five LSD and cocaine.

Roger Howard, chief executive of DrugScope, said: 'We are not surprised. The threat of criminal sanctions is simply not stopping large numbers of young people experimenting with drugs.'

Police forces already claim to have insufficient resources to monitor use of all drugs. The experiment in Lambeth introduced confiscation, rather than arrest for those found in possession of cannabis. Its pioneer, Commander Brian Paddick, has now been suspended after a former partner claimed he had smoked cannabis in Paddick's home.

Four out of five illegal drug users have taken cannabis, 27 per cent ecstasy, 25 per cent amphetamines and more than one in five LSD and cocaine

Under the scheme, arrests for dealing in hard drugs have climbed and street robberies have fallen.

Opponents of existing drugs laws say the illegality of cannabis and ecstasy in particular leads to the 'criminalisation' of otherwise law-abiding young people. Last year Prince Harry admitted taking cannabis while celebrating the end of his GCSEs.

The Home Affairs Select Committee is expected to recommend this summer that cannabis be decriminalised and ecstasy downgraded to Class B.

However, even as the Home Secretary wrestles with Britain's drugs crisis, he faces public pressure not to relax the drugs laws. Just 35 per cent of voters say cannabis should be decriminalised; 7 per cent want ecstasy made legal; only 4 per cent think all drugs should be freely available.

■ ICM Research polled 1,075 people aged 16-plus in February/March.
© *Guardian Newspapers Limited 2002*

Drug laws

Information from DrugScope

The Misuse of Drugs Act 1971

The laws controlling drug use are complicated. The Misuse of Drugs Act (MDA) regulates what are termed controlled drugs. It divides drugs into three classes as follows:

Class A: These include cannabis oil, cocaine and crack (a form of cocaine), ecstasy, heroin, LSD, methadone, processed magic mushrooms and any Class B drug which is injected.

Class B: These include amphetamine, barbiturates, cannabis (in resin or herbal form) and codeine.

Class C: These include mild amphetamines, anabolic steroids and minor tranquillisers.

Class A drugs are treated by the law as the most dangerous.

Offences under the Misuse of Drugs Act can include:

- Possession of a controlled drug.
- Possession with intent to supply another person.
- Production, cultivation or manufacture of controlled drugs.
- Supplying another person with a controlled drug.
- Offering to supply another person with a controlled drug.
- Import or export of controlled drugs.
- Allowing premises you occupy or manage to be used for the consumption of certain controlled drugs (smoking of cannabis or opium but not use of other controlled drugs) or supply or production of any controlled drug.

NB Certain controlled drugs such as amphetamines, barbiturates, methadone, minor tranquillisers and occasionally heroin can be obtained

through a legitimate doctor's prescription. In such cases their possession is not illegal.

The law is even more complicated by the fact that some drugs are covered by other laws, are not covered at all or treated in an exceptional way under the Misuse of Drugs Act.

Alcohol is not illegal for an over 5-year-old to consume away from licensed premises.

It is an offence for a vendor to knowingly sell to an under 18-year-old. A 14-year-old can go into a pub alone but not consume alcohol. A 16-year-old can buy and consume beer, port, cider or perry (but not spirits) in a pub if having a meal in an area set aside for this purpose. In some areas there are by-laws restricting drinking of alcohol on the streets at any age. Police also have powers to confiscate alcohol from under-18s who drink in public places.

GHB (gammahydroxybutyrate) is a colourless, odourless liquid which comes in a small bottle and has sedative and euphoric effects. It is not controlled under the Misuse of Drugs Act so possession is not an offence. It is classed as a medicine so unauthorised manufacture and supply could be an offence under the Medicines Act. However, this still allows the drug to be legally imported for personal use.

Ketamine usually comes as a powder. The initial rush is usually followed by feelings of dissociation and an anaesthetic-type experience. It is commonly used as an animal tranquilliser and for surgery on animals. Ketamine is not covered by the Misuse of Drugs Act and possession is not an offence. It is a prescription-only medicine under the Medicines Act meaning unauthorised supply is illegal.

Khat is a plant that is grown in eastern Africa and the Arabian peninsula. Chewing the leaves has a stimulant effect. Some Khat is imported to the UK and sold in

greengrocers', specialist health food shops and some 'head' shops. The Khat plant (the main form in which khat is sold) is not covered under the Misuse of Drugs Act and possession or supply is not an offence.

Magic mushrooms are not illegal to possess or eat in their raw state. It can be an offence to process them by drying and storing them, making them into a tea or infusion or cooking with them.

Of the 127,000 people who committed drug offences under the MDA in 1998 50 per cent were given a police caution and not taken to court

---

Poppers (liquid gold, amyl or butyl nitrite) are not covered by the MDA and are not illegal to possess or buy. They are often sold in joke and sex shops but also in some pubs, clubs, tobacconists and sometimes music or clothes shops used by young people. Though not fully tested in court, the Medicines Control Agency has stated that poppers are regarded by them as a medicine and so falls under the Medicines Act 1968. This allows only licensed outlets, such as chemists, to sell the drug.

Solvents (aerosols, gases, glues etc.) are not illegal to possess, use or buy at any age. In England and Wales it is an offence for a shopkeeper to sell them to an under 18-year-old if they know they are to be used for intoxicating purposes. The Government intends to extend this legislation to make it illegal for shopkeepers to sell lighter fuel (butane) to under-18s whether or not they know it will be used for intoxicating purposes.

Anabolic steroids are controlled under the Misuse of Drugs Act as Class C drugs but their legal status is complicated. In most situations the possession offence is waived meaning that people who possess or use steroids without a prescription are unlikely to be prosecuted. However, in some areas of the UK police have successfully prosecuted people for possession of steroids when the steroids have not been in the form of a medicinal product. It is always an offence to sell or supply steroids to another person. People can also be prosecuted for possession with intent to supply if they have large quantities of steroids without a prescription for them.

Tobacco

It is not an offence for people of any age to purchase or use cigarettes or other tobacco products. It is an offence for a vendor to sell tobacco products to someone they know to be under 16 years old. Police also have powers to confiscate tobacco products from under-16s who are smoking in public places.

Minor tranquillisers (librium, valium etc.) are controlled under the Misuse of Drugs Act as Class C drugs but the possession offence is waived so that it is not illegal to possess or use them without a prescription. It is an offence to sell or supply them to another person. The exception is temazepam and rohypnol tranquillisers which are illegal to be in possession of without a prescription.

Maximum penalties under the Misuse of Drugs Act are as follows:

Drug Class	Possession	Supply
A	7 years + fine	Life + fine
B	5 years + fine	14 years + fine
C	2 years + fine	5 years + fine

In 1998 over 127,000 people were processed for offences under the MDA. Of these people 89 per cent were male and 11 per cent were female. 6 per cent were under 17 years old, 28 per cent were 17 to 20, 21 per cent were 21-24, 20 per cent were 25-29 and 25 per cent were aged 30 and over.

What happens to people who commit drug offences varies in different parts of the UK

Of the 127,000 people who committed drug offences under the MDA in 1998:

- 50 per cent were given a police caution and not taken to court.
- 22 per cent were fined.
- 18 per cent were dealt with by other means such as suspended prison sentences, probation or supervision orders, community service orders or discharged.
- 9 per cent were imprisoned.

Almost 70 per cent of cases concern the possession of relatively small amounts of cannabis. This may result in a small fine but in many areas police will issue a caution (especially when it is a first offence involving young people) and not take the case to court. By 1992 over half of all drug offenders were receiving cautions and this trend has continued. A caution is noted by the police but does not count as a criminal record. It is a bit like a warning and is likely to lead to a prosecution if the offence is repeated.

In 1998 the percentage of offenders dealt with in various ways was as follows:

Method dealt with	Possession	Supply
Immediate custody	5%	45%
Fine	24%	5%
Other means	21%	40%
Cautioned	50%	9%

What happens to people who commit drug offences varies in different parts of the UK. Police forces in some areas are more likely to caution than in other areas. Some local police forces are more likely than others to charge people and take them to court. What happens in courts also varies. Some courts are more likely to give out custodial sentences or large fines than others.

Other drug laws

The Medicines Act 1968

This law governs the manufacture and supply of medicines. It divides medical drugs into three categories:

1. Prescription-only medicines are the most restricted. They can only be sold or supplied by a pharmacist if prescribed by a doctor.
2. Pharmacy medicines can be sold without a prescription but only by a pharmacist.
3. General Sales List medicines can be sold by any shop, not just a pharmacy. Even here advertising, labelling and production restrictions apply.

The enforcement of the Medicines Act rarely affects the general public.

Customs and Excise Management Act 1979

Together with the Misuse of Drugs Act, the Customs and Excise Act penalises unauthorised import or export of controlled drugs. The maximum penalties are the same as for other trafficking offences except that in a magistrates' court fines can reach up to three times the value of the drugs seized.

Road Traffic Act 1972

It is an offence to be in charge of a motor vehicle while 'unfit to drive through drink or drugs'. The drugs can include illegal drugs, prescribed medicines or solvents.

Drug Traffickers Offences Act 1994

It is an offence to sell articles for the preparation or administration of controlled drugs – such as cocaine snorting kits. The Act also allows for the seizure of assets and income of someone who is found guilty of drug trafficking, even if the assets and income cannot be shown to have come from the proceeds of drug trafficking.

Crime and Disorder Act 1998

This new Act introduces, for the first time, enforceable drug treatment and testing orders, for people convicted of crimes committed in order to maintain their drug use.

- The above information is from DrugScope's web site which can be found at www.drugscope.org.uk

© DrugScope

Our fight against drug smuggling

Information from HM Customs and Excise

Illegal drugs can touch the lives of everyone. You might be affected directly if you have a friend or a family member who is a drug user, or indirectly through having to live with the threat of drug-related crime.

Experts estimate the worldwide illegal drugs trade is worth as much as the individual oil, gas or world tourism industries. Whatever the true figure, the UK alone spends more than one billion pounds tackling the problem. Our Government is fighting back with a national anti-drugs strategy – *Tackling Drugs To Build A Better Britain* – in which HM Customs and Excise plays a key role.

It pulls together a host of anti-drugs initiatives set up to:

- help young people resist drug misuse and achieve their full potential
- protect our communities from drug-related anti-social and criminal behaviour
- enable people with drug problems to overcome them and live healthy and crime-free lives
- stifle the availability of illegal drugs on our streets.

Customs and Excise is channelling considerable anti-smuggling expertise into achieving this last goal.

Working with other agencies such as the police, National Criminal Intelligence Service and the National Crime Squad we are committed to:

- reducing the supply of illegal drugs
- dismantling the criminal gangs that traffic drugs
- helping our colleagues around the world tackle illegal drug production and distribution
- depriving traffickers of their assets and proceeds of crime.

Drug culture

UK law classifies some types of drugs as 'controlled' substances, which means it is illegal to import or export them, possess them, possess them with an intention to supply them to others, or actually supply them without a licence.

These drugs are split into three categories – Class A, B and C – according to the threat they pose to a person's health and to society as a whole:

- Class A drugs include those which are widely abused, such as heroin, cocaine and Ecstasy
- Class B drugs include cannabis and amphetamine
- Class C drugs include anabolic steroids and temazepam.

The most harmful drugs are heroin and cocaine, which are the top but not the sole priority of the national drugs strategy.

Overseas threat

Illegal drug manufacture of heroin and cocaine is almost unheard of in the UK.

Most of the drugs taken by British users come from thousands of miles away on different continents. They are shipped into our country by sophisticated chains of international criminals. For instance,

> *Experts estimate the worldwide illegal drugs trade is worth as much as the individual oil, gas or world tourism industries . . . the UK alone spends more than one billion pounds tackling the problem*

the majority of heroin sold in the UK started life as opium poppies in south-west Asia, in countries such as Pakistan and Afghanistan.

It is processed and moved to Turkey, before being shuttled to Britain through Europe.

Cocaine is similar. Its origins are more likely to be in South America. A great deal is routed through the Caribbean, stockpiled in Spain, Portugal, France, Belgium and the Netherlands before making it into the hands of British dealers.

The Low Countries of Belgium and the Netherlands also tend to be

prime sources of synthetic drugs, such as Ecstasy and amphetamine, although production appears to be on the rise in the UK, too.

The main source country for cannabis tends to be Morocco.

Smugglers and their techniques

Traffickers try a huge variety of scams to get past Customs officers. We routinely seize drugs that have been:

- swallowed or stuffed into a body cavity
- hidden on a person
- packed into someone's luggage or belongings
- stashed in a car, boat or aeroplane
- hidden in seemingly legitimate freight.

Drugs have only been controlled for a short period of time. But centuries of experience in dealing with smugglers has taught us where some of the biggest risks are and what to look out for.

Our officers develop detailed intelligence which helps us pinpoint smuggling attempts that follow unrecognised sea or air routes – yachts that dump huge bundles of drugs overboard in secluded coves, for instance.

A vital source of help is information from the public to our Customs Confidential Hotline or through C&E's close links to trade organisations.

Also, the Anti-Drugs Alliance is a valuable source of information. This is a partnership between Customs and more than 90 legitimate companies who do not want their

names tainted by the drugs trade.

The Alliance consists of more than 10,000 individuals from the shipping, freight-handling and vehicle hire industries. Their professional knowledge and assistance prove vital in catching and jailing drugs gangs.

Guns and violence

Some drugs gangs use the threat of extreme violence to protect their lucrative cargo. It's not just detection which threatens their shipments, but theft by rival criminals.

A kilo of heroin costs less than £1,000 in Pakistan but on British streets it is worth more than 75 times as much.

This potential profit has drawn major organised crime syndicates to drug smuggling – the Mafia and Jamaican Yardies are known to be involved.

But trafficking also carries massive risks, including some of the most severe international legal penalties.

This means that some drug traffickers are violent and carry guns. It means our officers – who are

unarmed – have to work closely with armed police specialists to stop these potentially ruthless criminals.

Our officers

Tackling Class A drug smuggling is one of Customs' top priorities. Units of specialist investigators and dedicated anti-smuggling teams at ports and airports focus solely on tackling illegal drug activities.

But it isn't just on land we operate. Britain's coastline is guarded by Customs and Excise's seven ships called cutters. Nor is it just humans involved in the anti-trafficking effort. Our sniffer dogs have recorded enormous successes throughout their decades of service.

The most severe penalties

Criminals convicted of trafficking large amounts of Class A drugs risk spending the rest of their lives in jail.

Smuggling Class B drugs carries a 14-year maximum sentence, while Class C substances have a seven-year limit.

But we don't just aim to jail smugglers. Our officers make great efforts to have them stripped of their ill-gotten assets and money. It is one of our contributions to the national drugs strategy.

We also seize any cash that we discover being moved in or out of the country and that we can prove is connected to trafficking offences.

■ The above information is from HM Customs and Excise's web site which can be found at www.hmce.gov.uk
© Crown copyright

Your rights on arrest

You have the right to be treated fairly and with respect by the police. You do not have to say anything to the police. But if you are later charged with a crime and you have not mentioned, when questioned, something that you later rely on in court, then this may be taken into account when deciding if you are guilty. There may be good reasons why you do not wish to say anything to the police, and you should not be intimidated into answering questions. Get a solicitor down to see you in the police station as soon as possible.

Remember:

There may be times when if you give an innocent explanation for what you have done, the police may leave you alone.

- It is wise not to discuss the case with the police until you have consulted privately with a solicitor.
- If the police are about to arrest you or have already arrested you, there is no such thing as a 'friendly chat' to sort things out. Anything you say can later be used against you. Think before you talk.

When the police get it wrong

If you want to challenge anything the police have done then get the names and addresses of any witnesses, make a written record as soon as possible after the event. It should be witnessed, dated and signed. If you are injured, or property is damaged, then take photographs or video recordings as soon as possible and have physical injuries medically examined. If you have been treated unfairly then complain to a civil liberties group such as Release or contact a solicitor about possible legal action.

On the street

If you are stopped by the police:

- If they are not in uniform then ask to see their warrant card.
- Ask why you have been stopped and at the end ask for a record of the search.
- You can be stopped and searched if the police have a reasonable suspicion that you are in possession of:
- controlled drugs
- offensive weapon or firearms
- carrying a sharp article
- carrying stolen goods
- if you are in a coach or train, going to, or you have arrived at, a sports stadium.

There are other situations where you can be stopped and searched, for example:

- If police fear there might be serious violence in a particular area they can stop and search anyone in that area for up to 24 hours. In these circumstances the police do not need to have a reasonable suspicion that you are carrying a weapon or committing a crime. This very wide power can be used at raves, demonstrations etc.

Remember:

You run the risk of both physical injury and serious criminal charges if you physically resist a search. If it is an unlawful search you should take action afterwards by using the law.

In a police station

You always have the right:

- to be treated humanely and with respect.
- to see the written codes governing your right and how you are treated.
- to speak to the custody officer (the officer who must look after your welfare).
- to know why you have been arrested.

You also have the right (but it can in rare situations be delayed):

- to have someone notified of your arrest (not to make a phone call yourself).
- to consult with a solicitor privately.

Remember:

Do not panic. You cannot be locked up indefinitely. The police sometimes keep you isolated and waiting in the cell to 'soften you up'. Above all else, try to keep calm. The police can only keep you for a certain period of time – normally a maximum of 24 hours (36 hours for a serious arrestable offence).

Make sure the correct time for your arrest is on the custody record. Make sure you know why you have been arrested. Insist on seeing a solicitor (you might have to wait, but it's always free). Ask them to be present when you are interviewed. Do not be put off seeing a solicitor by the police. It is your right, and it's free.

If you ask for anything and it is refused make sure this is written down on the custody record.

Search of your home

- The police can search premises with the consent of the occupier.
- A warrant can obtained from magistrates by the police to search premises for evidence of certain crimes.
- The police can enter premises WITHOUT a search warrant in many situations, including:
  – following an arrest, the police are allowed to search premises the detained person occupies or has control over.
  – to capture an escaped prisoner.
  – to arrest someone for an arrestable offence or certain public order offences.
  – to protect life or to stop serious damage to property.
  – other laws give police specific powers to enter premises.

Remember:

You are entitled to see a copy of any search warrant.

Police can use reasonable force to gain entry.

Police should give you information about their powers to search premises.

A record of the search must be kept by the police.

You or a friend should be allowed to be present during the search but this right can be refused if it is thought it might hinder investigations.

- The above information is from Release's web site: www.release.org.uk

© Release

Government to cut sentences for drug dealers

The Christian Institute today voiced alarm at the Home Secretary's plans for going soft on cannabis and downgrading the drug from Class B to C. Leaks to the effect that there will be 'longer jail sentences for cannabis dealers' are totally untrue. The maximum sentences are to be cut from what they are now.

'Cannabis is a gateway drug. We fear that thousands more children will become hooked on hard drugs thanks to this policy change'

Colin Hart, Director of The Christian Institute, said today: 'The Government is going soft on cannabis. The result will be open cannabis dealing and cannabis smoking on the streets. This has already happened in Lambeth, where a softer policing experiment has seen children as young as ten being found openly smoking the drug.

'Reclassifying cannabis sends out the message to young people that taking cannabis is OK. Abstruse arguments about whether it is decriminalisation will be lost on young people. Cannabis is a

THE CHRISTIAN INSTITUTE

CHRISTIAN INFLUENCE IN A SECULAR WORLD

gateway drug. We fear that thousands more children will become hooked on hard drugs thanks to this policy change.

'Taking drugs is wrong. We ought to be sending out this message to young people rather than undermining parents who want to keep their kids away from drugs.

'Downgrading cannabis to Class C puts cannabis in the same category as sleeping pills where the police give very little priority to law enforcement. Home Office figures show that in 2000 only 4.3kg of all Class C drugs were seized (about the weight of four bags of sugar) compared to 46,893kg of Class B drugs (93% of this was cannabis).

'The Government have just appointed 950 Customs Officers to tackle tobacco smuggling at the same time as telling Customs Officers not to target cannabis smuggling. The Government are open to the charge that they are less bothered about cannabis than loss of tobacco revenue.

'Currently the maximum prison sentence for dealing in Class 'B' drugs is 14 years. For Class 'C' drugs the maximum is 5 years. Tinkering with the legislation and making the penalty 10 years for dealing in cannabis at Class C still means less time in jail for drug dealers.

'Reclassifying cannabis will also hamstring the police. Even if the Home Secretary empowers police to arrest for Class C possession where there are "aggravating factors", this will still leave the police powerless in most cases. At the moment the police can arrest for a cannabis offence whenever they see fit.

'Greater use of on-the-spot fines for cannabis possession has always been an option ever since last year when Parliament passed the legislation. The fact is, the Home Secretary can keep cannabis as a Class B drug and introduce on-the-spot fines at the same time.

'In some areas the penalty for dropping litter is £50. On-the-spot fines for cannabis must be substantially higher than £50. Otherwise, this raises the ludicrous prospect of a cannabis user getting a larger fine for dropping his joint in the street than for smoking it. Also, there must be greater sanctions for repeat offences.'

An online version of *Going soft on cannabis*, The Christian Institute's briefing booklet on cannabis, is available at www.christian.org.uk

■ The above information is from The Christian Institute's web site: www.christian.org.uk

© The Christian Institute

'The Government is going soft on cannabis. The result will be open cannabis dealing and cannabis smoking on the streets'

Cannabis

The reclassification of cannabis

Before – Class B	After – Class C
14-year prison sentence (max.) for cannabis dealing	5 years (or 10 if press speculation is correct)
Cannabis in same class as amphetamines	Cannabis in same class as sleeping pills
Police have power of arrest	No power of arrest. But if press speculation correct, the police may be given power in exceptional circumstances.
Possible on-the-spot fines	Possible on-the-spot fines

Seizures of illegal drugs in 2000

	Class B	Class C
Seizures in 2000	93,321 seizures	1,902 seizures
Weight seized in 2000	46,893kg	4.3kg

The reclassification of cannabis

A summary of the report on the reclassification of cannabis

Why and how are illegal drugs 'classified'?

The classification of illegal drugs is based on the harm that they may cause. In advising on the harmfulness of drugs, the council takes into account the physical harm that they can cause, their pleasurable effects, associated withdrawal reactions after chronic (heavy) use and the harm that misuse may bring to families and to society.

What are the levels of cannabis use in the UK?

Cannabis use appears to have increased dramatically over the last 20 years. Local and national surveys tell us that cannabis use is highest amongst 16- 29-year-olds, and it is more commonly used by males rather than females. There is considerable use in both urban and rural parts of the UK, and also use is spread across a broad range of users, regardless of educational background or social standing. The number of cannabis offences is often used as a good indicator of levels of cannabis use in the UK, and there has been an increase from 15,388 offences in 1981, to 99,140 in 1998

What are the health risks associated with cannabis use?

The health risks of cannabis use are split into two; these are the acute effects and the long-term effects.

Acute health risks

Acute health risks are those which affect the user immediately after using cannabis. Cannabis leads to the dilation of some blood vessels and the constriction of others. The dilation (widening) of the conjunctival blood vessel leads to what is commonly known as 'red eye', while the constriction (tightening) of other blood vessels leads to an increase in blood pressure. Cannabis

also produces an increase in heartbeats per minute, similar to the effects of exercise, and probably does not pose a significant risk to the heart in healthy, young people. However, those who have any sort of heart condition should be aware that the effects of cannabis on them could be dangerous. Cannabis use can worsen asthma and may decrease sperm counts and mobility in males while possibly suppressing ovulation in women. Cannabis use does affect your ability to perform complex tasks that require sustained attention, and when this involves operating heavy machinery or driving, using cannabis is dangerous. However, unlike alcohol, using cannabis does not seem

to increase risk-taking behaviour. This is probably why it seems to play a smaller role than alcohol in road traffic accidents. Cannabis use rarely contributes to violence, whereas alcohol use is a major factor in deliberate self-harm, domestic accidents and violence. Heavy cannabis intoxication can lead to panic attacks, paranoia and confused feelings, that can drive users to seek medical help, and can also produce a psychotic state in the user. People who have a mental illness, especially schizophrenia, should avoid cannabis use as it can unquestionably worsen their condition.

Long-term risks

As most cannabis users will smoke it mixed with tobacco, cannabis does present a significant health risk. It can increase the likelihood of the user developing bronchitis, asthma and lung cancer, as well as disorders of the heart and circulation. In addition to this, cannabis may be

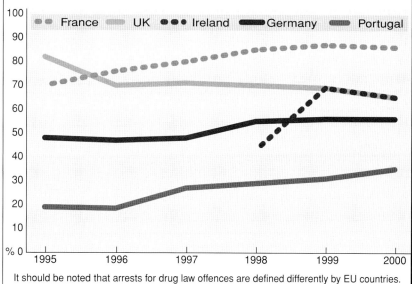

Cannabis among total of drug use/possession arrests

In some countries cannabis is the substance involved in most offences of drug use or possession

Legend: France · · · · · UK · ● ● ● Ireland · ━━━ Germany · · · · · Portugal

It should be noted that arrests for drug law offences are defined differently by EU countries.

Source: 2001 Reitox national reports

more dangerous than tobacco, as it has a higher concentration of certain carcinogens (chemicals that cause cancer). Some severe cases of lung damage have been reported in very young, heavy cannabis users. In terms of dependency (relying heavily on the drug day to day) this has been confirmed as a real issue, with 5-10% of people who use drug treatment services giving cannabis as their main problem drug. Heavy users who stop may well experience a physical withdrawal, which includes a loss of appetite, weight loss, lethargy (tiredness), irritability, mood changes and insomnia (not being able to sleep). While there is not a physical craving for cannabis, there can be a psychological craving for it. Therefore, repeated use of cannabis does lead to a high percentage of users becoming dependent on the drug, yet unlike heroin or crack, the level of their dependence on the drug will usually not lead to criminal behaviour.

Cannabis use in pregnancy is not safe, but it is probably no more dangerous to the foetus than either alcohol or tobacco. All of these drugs should be avoided throughout the duration of the pregnancy.

The gateway theory suggests that cannabis use leads people to progress on to other drug use, as in previous studies, heroin and crack users have been found to have used cannabis first. Many have claimed that cannabis is the main factor in their progression to these potentially life-threatening drugs. However, this ignores the fact that most Class A drug users will have probably tried alcohol and tobacco before cannabis, and also ignores the fact that the user's personality and environment can influence an individual's choice to use Class A drugs.

Cannabis use does cause harm, and its use does present risks to both the individual and to society. However, cannabis is less harmful than other substances in the current Class B category

---

What changes will the proposed reclassification of cannabis lead to?

Levels of use (prevalence)

Many people believe that the reclassification would lead to an increase in use of cannabis. But reclassification is not the same as decriminalisation or legalisation, and if the reclassification takes place, then penalties, including imprisonment would, still remain. The only change would be the reduction of the maximum penalty for the use or supply of cannabis i.e. a person found guilty of supplying cannabis would face a maximum penalty of 5 years rather than 14 years.

If the drug is reclassified, then the Advisory Council for the Misuse of Drugs will continue to monitor the prevalence of cannabis use.

Policing and law enforcement

Reclassifying cannabis would mean that personal possession of the drug would no longer be an 'arrestable' offence in England and Wales. However, the police will still have separate powers of arrest under section 25 of the PACE act (see Cascade homepage for details).

Treatment

There is anecdotal evidence (word of mouth) that cannabis users do not access drug treatment services, as they feel that their problem will not be taken seriously. Therefore, it is important that efforts are made to provide good public health information about cannabis and it's potential for dependency, and that treatment services can provide assistance for those with cannabis dependency problems.

Education

It is important that if cannabis is reclassified, then the decision and the reasons for it are properly understood. Cannabis is a harmful drug, and therefore, the provision of accurate and impartial advice on the effects of cannabis must be an important part of the UK's drug strategy.

Even if this gateway theory is correct, then it cannot be a very wide gate, as the majority of cannabis users do not move on to Class A drugs.

There is a distinct possibility that the main factor in an individual choosing to use Class A drugs is the personality of the individual, and the peer group (family and friends) with whom the individual is involved. However, the one way in which cannabis use may lead to the use of Class A drugs is through the shared illegal drug market. For example, a cannabis dealer may also sell ecstasy, cocaine, heroin or crack, and in exposing themselves to cannabis the buyer may also be exposed to these drugs. To highlight this, the lower level of heroin use in the Netherlands (where cannabis can be bought from coffee shops legally) as opposed to the UK is claimed to be due to the separation of the cannabis and heroin markets.

Conclusions

Cannabis use does cause harm, and its use does present risks both to the individual and to society. However, cannabis is less harmful than other substances in the current Class B category. This is misleading, as users may think that the harmful effects of cannabis are similar to the harmful effects of other Class B drugs, such as amphetamine (speed). They may believe that since cannabis has had no major harmful effects on their health, then other Class B drugs will be equally safe. Therefore, the Advisory Council for the Misuse of Drugs recommends the reclassification of all cannabis preparations (resin, weed, skunk, oil etc.) to Class C under the Misuse of Drugs Act 1971.

■ The above information is an extract from Cascade's web site: www.cascade-drugs.org.uk

© Cascade

Government proposals on cannabis

Q. Is cannabis going to be legalised?

A. No. On 10 July 2002 the Home Secretary proposed that cannabis should be reclassified from a Class B to a Class C drug under the Misuse of Drugs Act. If approved by Parliament, this will give cannabis the same legal status as illegally obtained steroids or other prescription drugs such as tranquillisers. This will reduce the maximum penalty for possession of cannabis from 5 years' to 2 years' imprisonment.

Q. Why might the law on cannabis be changed?

A. The Government wants to free up police time to tackle serious drug crime and to emphasise the enormous risks associated with Class A drug use. It believes that the current classification of cannabis undermines the credibility of this message particularly amongst young people. However, the Government does not want the significant, but less serious, risks associated with using cannabis to be overlooked either.

Q. Is cannabis safe?

A. No. Cannabis use (particularly frequent use) can result in short-term memory loss and loss of concentration. Young people using cannabis are more likely to have accidents or get into situations they do not feel able to control. In the longer term, smoking cannabis damages respiratory function and is linked to lung cancer (in much the same way as cigarettes). Continued use can result in serious psychological dependence and mild withdrawal

Young people using cannabis are more likely to have accidents or get into situations they do not feel able to control

symptoms. It can also cause psychotic reactions amongst individuals with mental health problems. The medical benefits of some of the chemicals found in cannabis (but not cannabis itself) are being investigated.

Q. When will the law change?

A. If approved by Parliament, the new legislation could be in force by July 2003. But it is important to emphasise that possession of cannabis is illegal, and will remain so after any change to the legislation.

Q. If the law changes what will happen to a young person found with small amounts of cannabis?

A. As now, in the majority of cases the drug will be confiscated and the young person will receive a reprimand or warning. Arrest followed by

Dealing to minors will become a serious offence and those dealing near schools will be sentenced severely

a final warning or court appearance would apply in certain cases, such as for repeat offences, failing to provide a correct name and address, or smoking in a public place.

Please note the situation in Scotland is different – the drug will be seized as evidence, you may be charged with the offence and the matter will be reported to the Procurator Fiscal who will determine if a prosecution is in the public interest or if a fiscal fine or warning would be more suitable (for more information, please refer to www.knowthescore.info).

Q. What about dealers?

A. The Government is also proposing to protect the young by clamping down on those dealers who prey on them. Dealing to minors will become a serious offence and those dealing near schools will be sentenced severely.

■ The above information is from National Drugs Helpline's web site which can be found at www.ndh.org.uk

© *Department of Health, Crown copyright*

The liberalisation of cannabis

Route to a dead end. By David Partington

'If the war against drugs is lost then so are the wars against, theft, speeding, incest, fraud, rape, murder, arson and illegal parking. Few, if any, wars are winnable. So let us do anything we choose.'

Theodore Dalrymple

Theodore Dalrymple's words go a long way to helping us recognise the distorted logic that is behind many of the arguments trotted out ad infinitum by those who would relax our drug laws. Having been involved in helping people with addiction problems for 22 years I've certainly examined them over and over again looking for anything, anything which will prevent the heartache and despair caused by intoxicating substances like cannabis. Yet having spent all this time living and working with hundreds who began by using cannabis, as their entry into addiction, I feel there are fatal flaws inherent in what are, at first sight, such plausible and persuasive words.

The freedom to do what you want with your own body for instance is, at first sight, perfectly reasonable. For the people I and others worked with this was the very rationale that was used to persuade them it was OK to use drugs. 'If it feels good, do it' sounds very acceptable, especially when you're being told what a 'buzz' you're missing and all you have to do is take a puff of the joint a friend is offering. Yes, they knew it was wrong, not least because it was illegal, but in counselling they shared too, simply and quietly, that that it wasn't only the buzz that drew them to use more and more cannabis. It was the fact that the drugs cushioned them from a deep emptiness inside. They shared how that emptiness and despair came from emotional deprivation – from a lack of love and acceptance from parents who, if they were there at all, were often all too ready to make it

clear that they were something of a nuisance especially when they didn't achieve and meet their expectations. As their family and society increasingly rejected them the drug subculture they were increasingly moving in offered them a very real sense of community and belonging. Here, in an atmosphere of positive affirmation of their negative and damaging behaviour, they found their usage of drugs easily increasing.

There are those who mean well by suggesting that handing cannabis and other drugs out like aspirin would save people from degradation and a criminal record. Yes, but at what cost?

Once every Friday night had, long ago, become every Friday, Saturday, Sunday, Monday etc. and was used far more than once a day. And when they needed a bigger hit then the same dealer who provided them with cannabis was more than ready to offer them the other drugs he supplied.

Any presuppositions I may have had before going to Yeldall Manor about the type of person who might use drugs was very soon wiped away. Here were highly intelligent and gifted men whose full potential had been lost. Whose health had been dramatically affected, whose families had been devastated as they slid into full-scale addiction. Along the way they lost their friends through overdoses etc., friends who are part of the countless thousands who are no statistics, good or bad. There are those who mean well by suggesting that handing cannabis and other drugs out like aspirin would save people from degradation and a criminal record. Yes, but at what cost to those extra thousands and tens of thousands who become addicted because the government flash the green light which says it's

OK to be stoned. Slavery was banned years ago and even one extra life, enslaved to drugs on the altar of libertarianism, permissiveness and self-interest, is one too many. The judgement of history is quite clear about those societies, which encouraged the pursuit of self-indulgence and self-gratification at the expense of those who were vulnerable to negative influences.

Alongside the right to demean and enslave ourselves there is also the right to be protected from harm and self-harm by those stronger than ourselves

---

Of course we believe in the right to do what we like with our own bodies but alongside the right to demean and enslave ourselves there is also the right to be protected from harm and self-harm by those stronger than ourselves. I believe this includes the responsibility that we have to protect the young and the vulnerable from drug abuse. For those intoxicating substances which threaten their long-term well-being, their health and vitality, their God-given potential in every area of life.

We stand at a crossroads. One way goes the way the liberalisers would have us go which means society rolling over and surrendering this and future generations to the baser instincts we know we are all prone to. The other road costs much more, especially politically. It's the way of self-sacrifice where we surrender our right to some freedom for the sake of those more vulnerable and less informed.

I've seen enough ex-addicts find real freedom through taking the second road. They found liberty and freedom by acknowledging the fact that self-gratification and indulgence is second best. In an environment of acceptance and discipline they had the guts, the courage to face themselves as they really were and, often painfully, go through the discomfort of putting others first. But, in doing

so, they found their deepest needs being met for the first time in their lives.

I'm really not sure than most people will understand what on earth I'm talking about and would rather listen to the voices that promise heaven on earth through self-indulgence. I have certainly not heard from this House the voice of those who appear to have the political will to take the very tough choices necessary for the sake of the next and future generations. Sadly political expediency seems to reign alongside the increasing voice of commercial self-interest as over the Formula One Motor saga. As ever, history will judge this same House, but I really do pray it will not be at the expense of your children and

grandchildren as well as the countless thousands who say no to cannabis. Not because they have high ideals, because we haven't taught them many of those, but simply because the law gives them the boundaries which help them to abstain and, with it, the potential to become all they were created to become.

■ Dave Partington is the General Secretary of ISAAC (International Substance Abuse and Addiction Coalition).

■ The above information is from a collection of papers presented at a Consultation held in the Moses Room at the House of Lords on 28 November 2002.

© The Maranatha Community

Questions and answers about cannabis

1. Is cannabis addictive?
Some people become psychologically addicted – that means that the user gets into the habit of using it again and again. There are reports that some people when they stop taking the drug can also feel sick and irritable.

2. Is cannabis illegal?
Yes, personal use and supply are criminal offences. Possession means having cannabis on you, supply means giving it to other people – this includes passing a joint to a friend without them paying for it. People do go to prison for supplying cannabis.

3. Is cannabis a painkiller?
At the moment cannabis is not recognised as a painkiller. However, if clinical trials taking place in the UK pass all the tests then doctors may prescribe it. Remember – no medicine prescribed for us today is smoked.

4. Is cannabis safer than tobacco?
No, cannabis is not safer than tobacco e.g. the risk of lung, throat, or mouth cancer. It carries the same health risk as tobacco. However, cannabis has a higher tar content so you could develop diseases quicker.

5. Is it true that all young people use cannabis?
No, it is not true. In the year 2000 – 88% of all 11- to 15-year-olds had not used cannabis (Office for National Statistics 2001). According to ONS more boys than girls use cannabis.

6. If I want to stop using cannabis where can I go for help?
For more information on getting help you can contact Hope UK on 020 7928 0848 or the National Drugs Helpline on freephone 0800 776 600.

■ The above information is from Hope UK's web site which can be found at www.hopeuk.org

© Hope UK

Legalising drugs will save lives

Parents at the sharp end of drugs tragedies have taken a courageous stand against laws that harm, argues a leading campaigner for legalisation in response to Susan Greenfield's *Observer* commentary

A couple of weeks ago I got a call from Dave Hoskins. His son died a couple of years ago after taking ecstasy. After his son's death, Dave embarked on a publicity campaign in his town that involved standing outside clubs with a poster-sized picture of his son, warning against the dangers of drugs. He had also teamed up with Paul Betts – father of Leah who had also died after taking E. It would be an understatement to say that legalisation was not his preferred option for controlling drugs.

He had rung to speak to me after seeing the evidence session to the Home Affairs Committee (HAC) inquiry into UK drug policy, in which my colleagues and I had argued for the legalisation, control and regulation of drugs. As a result of seeing our evidence Dave had decided to back our calls for legalisation.

This is an astonishing turn-around for a man who has undergone the horror of the experience of the death of his child.

By Danny Kushlick

Until his son's death from a heroin overdose, Fulton Gillespie was a student of the 'hang 'em and flog 'em' school of drug policy. He now believes that a legalised system of heroin distribution might have saved his son's life.

Those of us calling for legalisation, control and regulation wish to see the criminal elements removed from the business

Mary Smith is a founder of Knowle West Against Drugs (KWADS). KWADS was one of the first community-led mothers against drugs groups to be set up in the UK. It is now one of the premier street drug agencies in Bristol. Mary's son was a problematic heroin user and a major pain in the arse for his mum and the community in which they lived. For years I debated the merits of legalisation with Mary while she pointed out the error of my ways. She recently announced that she was now supporting legalisation as the most sensible way of dealing with drugs in her community.

I have nothing but respect for the way that these individuals have come around, overcoming their hurt, anger and grief to take on a position of pragmatic harm reduction. It is their willingness to accept the reality of drug use and misuse that underlies their respective positions.

The fantasists

On the other side Professor Susan Greenfield, Melanie Phillips, Peter Hitchens and Clare Gerada (spokesperson for the Royal College of GPs) appear to inhabit a fantasy world

> *We have a stark choice: accept the reality of drugs in an adult fashion and manage the drugs market, or deny it and abrogate control to unregulated dealers and gangsters*

where young people can be persuaded to spend their hours playing hoopla and tinkering with the mechanisms of their fob watches. Professor Greenfield asked in last week's *Observer* 'Do we really want a drug culture lifestyle in the UK?' My dear professor, we already have one. And it cannot be stopped.

Although cannabis is at the more benign end of this culture, it cannot be denied that cannabis can be used dangerously. And, yes professor, it does 'make you see the world in a different way' and does literally 'leave its mark on how our neurons are wired up'. That is why people smoke it. And this is exactly why we must control and regulate its production and distribution. No drug is made safer left in the hands of organised criminals and unregulated dealers. Those of us calling for legalisation, control and regulation wish to see the criminal elements removed from the business and the end of the deregulation of the production and distribution of powerful psychoactive drugs. Cannabis (and indeed all drugs) must be legalised not because it is safe, but precisely because it is potentially dangerous.

It's prohibition what done it

Professor Greenfield spuriously asserts that the argument for legalising drugs is analagous to legalising mugging or burglary. Both these activities have a direct negative effect on other people. Stealing other people's property is a substantively different activity than rewiring one's neurons and does not warrant comparison.

Those who argue that drugs cause crime forget that it is the very policy of prohibition (not the use of the drugs themselves) that creates illegal drug markets and the property crime committed by problematic users. In his evidence to the HAC, Terry Byrne of Customs and Excise (C&E) gave the biggest clue as to why prohibition creates the very problems it is intended to solve. When asked if the efforts of C&E affected the price and availability of drugs at street level, he replied: 'Prices are as low as they have ever been. There is no sign that the overall attack on the supply side is reducing availability or increasing the price.' However, he did counter this with this comment on how C&E affects prices at wholesale level: 'The price of a kilo of cocaine in South America is £1000. It should cost about £1500 by the time it reaches the UK, but it actually costs £30, 000.' Herein lies a significant problem at the heart of prohibition – the thirtyfold increase in value of this illegally traded commodity. This may be a useful performance indicator for officials at Customs and Excise but the effects of this price hike are monumentally destructive. When combined with a huge level of demand, it makes the trade so lucrative that it becomes a magnet for organised crime. The UN estimates the value of the global trade at $400 billion a year (8% of international trade). The Home Office estimate for the UK is £6.6 billion. The amount of money involved is now so vast that no law enforcement agency can possibly halt the trade.

The massive premium added by Terry Byrne and his colleagues leads to the high price of heroin and cocaine at street level which is what fuels half of all shoplifting, burglary, vehicle crime and theft.

Withdrawing from prohibition

Our addiction to prohibition is based on a fantasy world in which our children can be kept safe from drug-related harm: through the UN Drug Control Programme's activities to stop Afghan farmers growing heroin, by talking up the dangers of cannabis, by locking up dealers and by showing pictures of dead young men and women.

Our children are not made safer as a consequence of prohibition; they are in fact in much more danger. From Bogata to Brixton prohibition is killing and causing untold misery to countless millions.

The fantasy of successful prohibition must end in order that we can see and engage with the reality of drug use in the twenty-first century.

Embracing a prohibition-free lifestyle

Legalisation is not a cure-all, however. Drug users young and old will still die as a result of using drugs and there will always be a small illegal market. We have a stark choice: accept the reality of drugs in an adult fashion and manage the drugs market, or deny it and abrogate control to unregulated dealers and gangsters.

Legalisation will produce a massive reduction in the problems surrounding drug use and create a context for an evidence-based analysis of what works in drug policy. The debate is being held back at present by a well-intentioned but misguided group of people who prefer the false safety of their fantasy (a world protected by prohibition) to facing up to the very real dangers of a society where illegal drugs are freely available with no controls at all.

There is nothing more dangerous than social policy built on escapist desires. It is never too late to relinquish the hold that prohibition has and embrace a prohibition-free lifestyle.

■ Danny Kushlick is director of Transform – the campaign for effective drug policy. www.transform-drugs.org.uk and www.tdpi.org.uk

■ This article first appeared in *The Observer*, 25 August 2002.
© *Transform Drug Policy Institute (TDPI)*

Legalising cannabis would be a 'historical mistake'

Information from the International Narcotics Control Board

Treating cannabis like alcohol and tobacco would be a 'historical mistake', the International Narcotics Control Board (INCB) states in its Annual Report 2002. While the damage to health caused by alcohol and tobacco is well known, it would be imprudent to add to the burden on national health care systems with another harmful substance like cannabis. The Board calls on all Governments and the relevant international bodies to review the situation and find ways to deal with developments on cannabis within the framework of international law.

The Board is increasingly concerned that some States which are signatories to the 1961 Single Convention on Narcotic Drugs, are circumventing the mandated controls of cannabis through legal manoeuvres. Cannabis, which is the most widely and frequently abused illicit drug in the world, is controlled under the 1961 Convention which has been ratified by 175 States. Most States are implementing the controls required under the Convention but some States are undermining the principle of the international drug control treaties which clearly state

that the use of drugs should be limited to medical and scientific purposes only.

Some Western European Governments have introduced legislation involving the decriminalisation of cannabis cultivation or possession for personal use. Four countries in the European Union (Italy, Luxembourg, Portugal and Spain) do not penalise the possession for personal use nor is it a criminal offence. The Board reaffirms its view that the 'coffee shops' in the Netherlands which sell cannabis products for non-medical use, contravene the 1961 Convention. The Board views the draft legislation on cannabis in Switzerland as a move towards the legalisation of the drug which would contravene the international drug control Conventions.

The Board is disturbed by the fact that while developing countries struggle to eradicate cannabis and fight illicit trafficking of the substance, certain developed countries have chosen to tolerate the cultivation, trade and abuse of cannabis on their territory. There is a growing gap between declared government policy and actual implementation of the treaties, which appears to be motivated by immediate domestic political priorities. The Board repeats its invitation to any Government if it believes there is scientific evidence that the control of cannabis under the 1961 Convention is not justified, to submit its evidence to the World Health Organization (WHO). Under the Convention, WHO is mandated to determine which substances are liable to abuse and should be under international control. Article 3 of the Convention has a specific mechanism for descheduling or rescheduling narcotic drugs and to ignore this procedure is to ignore established international law.

The Board believes that all efforts to control the world drug problem will fail unless there is universal commitment and true implementation of the provisions of the treaties.

The Board believes the likely increase in the abuse of cannabis and the harm to individuals and the community outweigh any possible benefits from relaxed controls on cannabis

---

The Board urges the international community to consider carefully the impact of amending cannabis controls on the international drug control system. The Board believes the likely increase in the abuse of cannabis and the harm to individuals and the community outweigh any possible benefits from relaxed controls on cannabis.

The Board also notes that, in line with its recommendations in earlier reports, a number of countries are evaluating the potential medical usefulness of cannabis. If the results of scientific research objectively show that cannabis is medically useful, it would still remain a substance to be strictly controlled, but which could be used for medical purposes, as is currently the case with other narcotic drugs.

■ The above information is from a press release produced by the International Narcotics Control Board. See page 41 for their address details.
© *International Narcotics Control Board*

Confusion on cannabis

Britain's rethink on cannabis is sending the wrong signal, says UN

Britain's 'softly softly' approach to cannabis is putting the health of a generation in peril, the United Nations has warned.

Its drugs watchdog says Home Secretary David Blunkett's decision to downgrade cannabis to a 'Class C' drug has caused 'confusion' and 'misunderstanding' all over the world.

Nine in ten children believe the drug is now legal in Britain, it says, while the public is being misled about the health risks.

The annual report of the International Narcotics Control Board (INCB), which monitors world drug markets and government policies, points to increasing evidence that marijuana can cause cancer, lung disease and abnormalities associated with mental illness.

Recent studies also suggest cannabis users are at least six times more likely than non-users to develop schizophrenia.

The report says Mr Blunkett's move caused 'worldwide repercussions . . . including confusion and widespread misunderstanding'.

It adds: 'A survey undertaken in the UK found that as many as 94 per cent of children believed that cannabis was a legal substance or even some kind of medicine. The survey also discovered that nearly 80 per cent of teachers believed the recent reclassification of cannabis would make educating pupils about the dangers of drug abuse more difficult.'

It says grave concerns about the international repercussions were raised at a recent meeting of the Heads of National Drug Law Enforcement Agencies of Africa.

'It was stated that the reclassification of cannabis by the UK would undermine the efforts of African countries to counter illicit cannabis cultivation, trafficking and abuse.

'That action, it was held, had sent the wrong message and could

By James Chapman,
Science Correspondent

lead to increased cultivation of cannabis destined for the UK.'

Control board president Dr Philip Emafo said yesterday that the public was being misled about the health risks.

'Advocated of drug legalisation are vocal and have access to considerable funds that are used to misinform the public,' he added. 'Cannabis is not a harmless drug as advocates of its legalisation tend to portray. 'Cannabis use affects the functioning of the brain.

'Its illicit use is also associated with heart attacks in some young people and can cause lung disease and cancer. It's important that consensus prevails in international drug control.

'No government should take unilateral measures without considering the impact on others.'

Board member Professor Hamid Ghodse, who also heads the addiction psychiatry department at St George's Hospital in London, warned that if cannabis use continued to increase there could be a huge rise in cannabis-related psychiatric cases in the next decade or two.

'Recreational use of cannabis is something that any government should think very seriously about,' he added.

'It is very odd that we are normalising cannabis use.

'We will have mental hospitals full of patients and a great deal of responsibility on our shoulders.'

Cannabis has become the most widely-used drug in the UK after alcohol and cigarettes. The number of teenage boys, for example, smoking it has rocketed in recent years.

In 1999, 19 per cent of boys aged 14 to 15 admitted they had tried cannabis. Two years later, that figure had risen dramatically to 29 per cent. Downgrading cannabis to a Class C drug means most users will not be arrested if caught with the drug.

Recent studies also suggest cannabis users are at least six times more likely than non-users to develop schizophrenia

Last night, a spokesman for the Home Office said the decision to do so was based on scientific evidence.

'We do not accept the INCB's statement that the decision to reclassify will lead to confusion and they are wrong to say that this sends a signal that we have decriminalised cannabis,' he said.

'Reclassification does not legalise cannabis but does make clear the distinction between cannabis and Class A drugs such as heroin, crack and cocaine – the drugs that cause the most harm to individuals and families, that tear apart communities and turn law-abiding citizens into thieves.

'Reclassification of cannabis allows the police to focus its resources on tackling the drugs that cause most harm.

'Cannabis is a harmful substance that still requires strict controls. That is why we intend to reclassify it as a Class C drug.'

© The Daily Mail
February 2003

What is effective drug policy?

Information from the Transform Drug Policy Institute (TDPI)

TRANSFORM DRUG POLICY INSTITUTE

Evidence suggests that attempts to prohibit drugs have been ineffective and are often counterproductive. Illegal drugs today are cheaper and more available than ever before, despite the billions spent each year attempting to control their supply and use. Drug misuse and associated problems of crime, illness and addiction, continue to rise and the UK now has the highest overall level of drug use in Europe.

Drugs are an emotive issue, with debate often dominated by scare-mongering rather than common sense. With the growing crisis being faced, there is an urgent need to look beyond the simplistic rhetoric of the 'war on drugs' and examine alternative drug policies that could be more effective. These include the possibility of replacing the existing prohibitionist framework with legally regulated drug markets.

An effective drug policy would

1) Regulate and control the drugs trade

Drug laws that seek to criminalise production, supply and use of drugs have never been successful in achieving their stated aims, however harshly they are enforced. The illegal market remains unregulated and out of our control.

There are a number of legal regulatory frameworks that exist for currently licensed drugs and medicines which allow control over production, price, quality, packaging and age of purchase. Given these legal options we must ask: Is there any benefit to giving monopoly control of this lucrative and dangerous market to organised crime and unregulated dealers?

2) Reduce drug-related ill health

Many of the health problems associated with illegal drugs are made far worse by their prohibition. Unknown strength and purity, poor information, and underfunded drug treatment all contribute to the dangers faced by drug users. Whilst rates of addiction, HIV and hepatitis continue to rise, the demonising and alienation of drug users means many are afraid to seek help. Moving towards a health rather than criminal justice focus for drug policy would allow us to help those in need and make all drug use safer.

3) Reduce drug-related crime

It is clear that the criminal drugs market – the direct consequence of prohibitionist laws – is the root of most of the crime associated with drugs. Unregulated dealers, gang violence and addicts committing property crime to fund their habits are just some of the problems attributable to the criminal market. Taking the trade out of the hands of criminals and putting it within a legal framework would help to eliminate the criminal market and its associated problems.

4) Maximise revenue and optimise expenditure

Government research shows that every pound spent on drug treatment saves £3 on criminal justice expenditure. Moving money away from policing and punishment and into care and rehabilitation is both compassionate and effective.

The global illegal drugs market is worth over £100 billion a year and rising – by far the biggest earner for modern-day Al Capones. A legally regulated market would keep profits within the legitimate economy and generate significant revenues for the treasury rather than for organised crime.

5) Extend the provision of honest and effective drugs education

Inadequate education is a major

factor contributing to the dangers of drug use (legal and illegal). Taboos around illegal drugs in particular have meant most education programmes have been misleading and in-effective. An expansion of drugs information services combined with a more realistic and balanced approach could address these short-comings.

6) Protect civil rights

For historical reasons some drugs are strictly prohibited whilst others are legally available. This illogical distinction criminalises millions in a way that is unjust and indiscriminate. Our basic rights to privacy and freedom of belief and practice are routinely infringed. In a modern society committed to civil rights we must accept all drug users have the same rights. With these rights come responsibilities, but when an individual's drug use is responsible and does not interfere with the rights of others, there is no justification for legal sanctions to be applied.

7) Deal with the underlying causes of drug misuse

The drug problem has historically been dealt with symptomatically with little attention paid to the underlying social problems that lead people to misuse drugs. Only by focusing on these underlying prob-lems (unemployment, bad housing, lack of opportunity, poverty, physical and emotional abuse) can we hope to significantly reduce the number of drug misusers.

8) Encourage involvement of communities

The negative impacts of prohibi-tionist drug policy are felt most heavily in deprived communities, where the prevalence of drug misuse is highest. These same communities are also the most excluded from the decision-making process, meaning policy rarely reflects their needs and aspirations. If we are serious about social inclusion we must allow people from all the affected communities, including drug users, a place at the policy-making table.

■ The above information is from the Transform Drug Policy Institute (TDPI). See page 41 for their contact details.

© Transform Drug Policy Institute (TDPI)

'Legalise all drugs now'

'Legalise all drugs now', says free market and civil liberties think-tank

While the Government's proposed decrim-inalisation of cannabis is a step in the right direction, full legalisation of all drugs must remain the final objective. So claims the Libertarian Alliance, Britain's most radical free market and civil liberties think-tank.

Libertarian Alliance spokesman, Dr Sean Gabb, said: 'We want a situation where any adult can go into a pharmacy and – without showing any permit or identification – buy as many drugs as he or she may want and use them for any self-regarding purpose. This means legalisation for recreational use and for self-medication.'

He added that nearly all the evils blamed on drugs can really be blamed on drug prohibition. For example:

■ Drug prohibition means that drugs are dangerous, because they are sold by dealers who have no concern for product safety;

■ Drug prohibition means that drugs are expensive, because the law requires them to be supplied by roundabout and uncompetitive means;

■ Drug prohibition breeds petty crime, because of the high price of drugs and the need to associate with criminals to get them;

■ Drug prohibition breeds organised crime, because of the large profits to be made from drugs once legitimate suppliers are driven from the market;

■ Drug prohibition breeds public corruption, as police and revenue officers, intelligence agencies, and politicians take bribes from organised crime to look the other way;

■ Drug prohibition leads to a war on freedom, because the only way of even trying to make prohibition work is to remove rights to privacy and due process – see, for example, the money laundering laws, and the 1997 bugging and burgling law, and the creeping in of asset forfeiture laws;

■ Drug prohibition brings the law into general contempt, because it criminalises private acts that in themselves cause no actionable harm to others, because it breeds corruption, and because it is actually unenforceable.

Of course, Dr Gabb added, as a libertarian, he believes that adults have an absolute right to do with themselves as they please, and this is independent of the utilitarian reasons given above.

The only answer, said Dr Gabb, is a return to 'Victorian Values' – the situation that existed in this country before the Dangerous Drugs Act 1920, when adults were free to decide for themselves what drugs to take and for what reason.

■ The Libertarian Alliance is Britain's most radical free market and civil liberties policy institute. It has published over 700 articles, pamphlets and books in support of freedom and against statism in all its forms.

■ The above information is from the Libertarian Alliance's web site which can be found at www.libertarian.co.uk

© The Libertarian Alliance

As long as drugs are illegal the problem won't go away

Addicts should be given drugs free so they don't have to mug and burgle

An air of wild unreality permeates most drug policy, so every glimmer of good sense among the nonsense is to be welcomed. Yesterday David Blunkett produced his new drugs strategy, which is a slight but important shift from his old drugs strategy. It targets the 250,000 hard drug users who cause most of the crime and social mayhem, costing 99% of the £10bn to £18bn a year officially guesstimated as the social cost of drugs. That is the right place to begin, but a target to treat just 200,000 of them by 2008 is hardly ambitious. Spending on treatment will rise by 40% by 2005 and it takes time to train people with the right skills. But this lacks a sense of crisis.

The worst estates, which Labour is dedicated to reviving through the New Deal for Communities, see heroin and crack as their deepest problem, both the cause and effect of their plight. The crack houses, the crime and drug-addicted prostitution, and the growing gun crime causes well-grounded terror among tenants. While a handful of middle-class children become addicts, hard drugs are an emblem of poverty, the final apocalypse that descends upon urban estates or wherever heavy industry vanishes and heavy drugs move in to fill the void of those deprived of significant work. Drugs campaigners often point to the success of Holland's drug policy where heroin users are a shrinking and aging group, kept well under control. But Dutch success may be due less to their drugs policy than to the good effect of a more equal society with an absence of gross poverty. Britain has the worst drugs problem in the EU because it has the most poverty.

Curing inequality may take time, but there is no excuse for Labour's still-rising prison population – due not to rising crime but to the

By Polly Toynbee

Straw/Blunkett punitive sentencing climate. Five years in office and Labour still has only half the addicts in prison under treatment, the very people who commit the crime and should be treated first. Although there will now be money, overcrowded prisons are bad places for doing good.

> More drugs are seized, yet the price of heroin and cocaine keeps falling, revealing how much keeps flowing in

Much of the double-think of drugs policy starts with the UN. It has a target to eradicate all cultivation of coca, cannabis and opium by the year 2008. 'A Drug Free World – We Can Do It!' is their dotty slogan. But for as long as dirt-poor countries can grow crops the rich world wants, they will. Considering the relative ease with which people traffickers get thousands of living, breathing humans across borders, small bags of drugs can never be prevented. More drugs are seized, yet the price of heroin and cocaine keeps falling, revealing how much keeps flowing in. Yet abject failure of drugs policies is met with calls for more of the same.

Some 90% of Britain's heroin comes from Afghanistan and the new drugs strategy blithely promises 'to reduce opium production and to eliminate it by 70% by 2008 and in full by 2013'. How? 'Improving security and law enforcement capacity and implementing reconstruction programmes which encourage

farmers away from poppy cultivation.' No details of how this miracle is to be accomplished were forthcoming, nor explanation of these random dates. Tony Blair gave Hamid Karzai's interim government £20m early this year to pay farmers not to plant opium, but to plant wheat. The farmers duly pulled up their crops, but they never received the money which stayed in the hands of the war lords. As a result they have now planted a double crop for this year.

The opium-growing areas are far beyond the reach of the Karzai government, whose writ does not run far. Why not? Because the West is now too preoccupied with Iraq: only this week at a meeting in Bonn the West again refused Karzai's plea for the 5,000-strong international force, ISAF, to be increased and deployed beyond Kabul to other cities. His own nascent army is neither ready nor equipped to keep order and his whole annual budget this year is only $460m: the West offered neither extra forces nor funds – so how is Karzai supposed to prevent opium growing? And why should it be a priority in a country with nothing else to export? Poor countries cannot and should not be expected to bear the brunt of rich countries' internal social failures. Colombia and growing numbers of other countries are being politically destabilised and destroyed as crime takes over, due to the impossible Western market that both demands drugs and outlaws them.

The contrariness of drug law is spelled out by Transform – the group that thinks only total decriminalisation of all drugs can stop the harm done by them. They pose a simple question: if you have a very dangerous substance, what is the best way of controlling it? Sell it over the counter (aspirins and tobacco), sell it in off-licences (alcohol), give it out in pharmacies on prescription (valium or temazepam) or give it to criminal gangs to dispense (heroin and crack)?

The real social danger of drugs comes from their prohibition which gives them to criminals and forces addicts to turn to crime to pay for it. Most people are not unduly worried about the welfare of the 250,000 addicts: 150,000 people die a year from smoking, which is their choice. The trouble with addicts is the huge volume of crime and violence they commit to support their habit. Eradicating drug abuse seems to make scant headway – but limiting the crime that addicts commit might work, by giving them the drugs free so they don't have to mug and burgle to get them.

At last the government is quietly inching along this road. They whisper it, it is tucked away in the new strategy. When asked, ministers are quick to say that only very few addicts will have heroin prescribed. But the Department of Health is now setting out to train large numbers of GPs in heroin prescribing so that addicts for whom all other treatments fail can be sustained safely and live orderly lives with their addiction. So far only 300 addicts can get heroin prescribed, but many more will now – and why not, if it reduces crime? Why not prescribe cocaine too, since crack addiction is exceptionally hard to cure? If drugs could be progressively eased out of the hands of the crime gangs as they have been in Holland where they are prescribed, then there is a chance of improvement. Improvement would be a triumph, while all talk of 'eradication' is destined for disappointment.

Meanwhile, down in the drug foothills, Blunkett retreated before the *Mail* on cannabis. First he downgrades it to Class C, but then he makes possession of any Class C drug potentially arrestable, which it was not before. Accept a sleeping pill from a friend and you could now be nicked. The police assure us that people will only be arrested for flagrant defiance – waving a sleeping pill in the face of an officer – but while there is local discretion, there will be local injustice. However, few doubt there will be a drastic cut in the current 90,000 arrests for cannabis possession. Little by little, things are getting more sensible.

© Guardian Newspapers Limited 2002

Cannabis poll

Q 1. The Home Secretary, David Blunkett, has recently announced that the possession of cannabis should no longer be an arrestable offence. From what you know, will this change mean that possessing cannabis is legal or illegal?

Possession legal	39%
Possession illegal	52%
Don't know	9%

Actually this change in the law means that possession of cannabis would remain illegal, but that users would not face prosecution

Q 2. Do you support or oppose this change in the law?

Support	50%
Oppose	39%
Don't know	11%

Q 3. Do you think people should be allowed to take cannabis, or not?

Should be allowed to take cannabis	42%
Should be allowed, but only for medical reasons	31%
Should not be allowed to take cannabis	24%
Don't know	3%

Q 4. Do you think this change in the law will lead to more people taking cannabis, fewer people taking cannabis, or do you think it will make no difference?

More people taking cannabis	43%
Fewer people taking cannabis	2%
Make no difference	53%
Don't know	2%

Q 5. The sale of cannabis should be legal but sold only through licensed government outlets

Strongly agree	35%
Tend to agree	30%
Neither	3%
Tend to disagree	11%
Strongly disagree	19%
Don't know	2%

Q 6. Using cannabis leads on to using harder drugs

Strongly agree	27%
Tend to agree	20%
Neither	6%
Tend to disagree	24%
Strongly disagree	17%
Don't know	6%

Q 7. Cannabis should be available on prescription to alleviate pain

Strongly agree	67%
Tend to agree	24%
Neither	2%
Tend to disagree	3%
Strongly disagree	4%
Don't know	0%

Q 8. Cannabis is worse for you than either alcohol or tobacco

Strongly agree	13%
Tend to agree	11%
Neither	14%
Tend to disagree	25%
Strongly disagree	20%
Don't know	17%

Q 9. If we reduce drugs use, crime rates will fall

Strongly agree	42%
Tend to agree	24%
Neither	5%
Tend to disagree	13%
Strongly disagree	12%
Don't know	4%

Q 10. Do you yourself use cannabis these days?
Q 11. And does anyone you know use cannabis these days?

	Q. 10	Q. 11
Yes	6%	33%
No	93%	66%
Don't know	1%	*
Refused	*	*

Q 12. And which of the following people you know use cannabis?

Partner	9%
Parents	4%
Brother/sister	12%
Other relative	17%
Work colleagues	35%
Friends	78%
Other	2%
Don't know	2%

Base: All who know someone who uses cannabis (200)

Q .12a And how likely is it that you will ever use cannabis in the future?

Certain to	*
Very likely to	1%
Quite likely to	5%
Not very likely to	28%
Certain not to	65%
Don't know	1%

Base: All who say they do not use cannabis (561)

A * indicates a finding of less than 0.5%, but greater than zero

Source: MORI

■ The proportion of 14- and 15-year-old boys who said they had tried the drug jumped from 19% in 1999, to 29% in 2001. (p. 01)

■ At 18, 63% of the sample had tried an illegal drug. By 23, this had risen to 76%. (p. 01)

■ The young people said their parents, too, were far more 'realistic' and tolerant of cannabis use than they were a few years ago. (p. 02)

■ The extent of drug use among 16- to 59-year-olds. The 2001/2002 *British Crime Survey* estimates that 34% of 16- to 59-year-olds have used an illicit drug at some time and 12% have used a Class A drug. Of all 16- to 59-year-olds, 12% had taken an illicit drug and 3% had used a Class A drug in the last year. This equates to around four million users of any illicit drug and around one million users of Class A drugs. (p. 04)

■ As in previous years, cannabis was the drug most likely to have been offered (27 per cent of pupils said they had been offered cannabis) but 22 per cent said they had been offered stimulants (a group of substances which includes cocaine and crack as well as ecstasy, amphetamines and poppers) and 20 per cent that they had been offered glue or gas.(p. 05)

■ In 2001, cannabis was by far the most likely drug to have been used – 13 per cent of pupils aged 11-15 had used cannabis in the last year. (p. 05)

■ Among 11- and 12-year-olds, misuse of volatile substances in the last year was more common than use of cannabis.(p. 05)

■ At least 45 million Europeans (18% of those aged 15 to 64) have tried cannabis at least once. (p. 07)

■ At present, most estimates for individual EU countries are between two and ten addicts per 1,000 population aged 15-54. (p. 08)

■ Teenagers who smoke cannabis are risking depression and schizophrenia later in life, three new studies conclude today. (p. 08)

■ Schools' zero tolerance policies towards drugs may be counter-productive because they encourage children to conceal drug problems, according to Home Office research. (p. 09)

■ 42% of young homeless people had taken heroin and 38% crack cocaine – about 20 times the average. (p. 09)

■ Comparing last year prevalence estimates for 16- to 59-year-olds from the 2000 *British Crime Survey* with those from the 2001/2002 sweep, there have been statistically significant decreases in the use of amphetamines, crack, heroin, LSD, magic mushrooms and steroids. However, over the same period there were statistically significant increases in the use of ecstasy.

■ The 250,000 class A drug users with the most severe problems who account for 99% of the costs of drug abuse in England and Wales and do most harm to themselves, their families and communities. (p. 17)

■ The main law controlling the use of drugs is the Misuse of Drugs Act. It divides drugs into three classes A-C. Class A drugs are regarded as the most dangerous and so carry the heaviest penalties. (p.18)

■ If you are going for a job interview, you may face a drug test, even if the job has nothing to do with public safety. (p. 19)

■ Four out of five illegal drug users have taken cannabis, 27 per cent ecstasy, 25 per cent amphetamines and more than one in five LSD and cocaine. (p.20)

■ More than half of Britain's 16- to 24-year-olds havetaken illegal drugs. (p.20)

■ Two in five people between 25 and 34 and more than a third of 35- to 44-year-olds say they have taken unlawful drugs. (p.20)

■ 'Currently the maximum prison sentence for dealing in Class 'B' drugs is 14 years. For Class 'C' drugs the maximum is 5 years. (p.26)

■ The number of cannabis offences is often used as a good indicator of levels of cannabis use in the U.K., and there has been an increase from 15,388 offences in 1981, to 99,140 in 1998. (p. 28)

■ 'A survey undertaken in the UK found that as many as 94 per cent of children believed that cannabis was a legal substance or even some kind of medicine. (p. 35)

■ In 1999, 19 per cent of boys aged 14 to 15 admitted they had tried cannabis. Two years later, that figure had risen dramatically to 29 per cent. (p. 35)

■ Some 90% of Britain's heroin comes from Afghanistan. (p. 38)

ADDITIONAL RESOURCES

You might like to contact the following organisations for further information. Due to the increasing cost of postage, many organisations cannot respond to enquiries unless they receive a stamped, addressed envelope.

Care for the Family
PO Box 488
Cardiff, CF15 7YY
Tel: 029 2081 0800
Fax: 029 2081 4089
E-mail: mail@cff.org.uk
Web site: www.care-for-the-family.org.uk
Committed to strengthening family life, and helping those who are hurting because of family break-up.

Cascade
Keepers Lodge, Chelmsley Road, Chelmsley Wood
Solihull, West Midlands, B37 7UA
Tel: 0121 788 3436
Fax: 0121 779 1701
E-mail: theteam@cascade-drugs.org.uk
Web site: www.cascade-drugs.org.uk
A drug information service for young people, parents and professionals.

The Christian Institute
26 Jesmond Road
Newcastle Upon Tyne, NE2 4PQ
Tel: 0191 281 5664
Fax: 0191 281 4272
E-mail: info@christian.org.uk
Web site: www.christian.org.uk
Works to promote the Christian faith in the United Kingdom.

DrugScope
Waterbridge House
32-36 Loman Street
London, SE1 0EE
Tel: 020 7928 1211
Fax: 020 7928 1771
E-mail: services@drugscope.org.uk
Web site: www.drugscope.org.uk
The UK's leading independent centre of expertise on drugs.

European Monitoring Centre for Drugs and Drug Addiction (EMCDDA)
Rua da Cruz de Santa Apolónia 23-25
PT-1149-045 Lisboa, Portugal
Tel: + 351 21 811 3032
Fax: + 351 21 813 1711
E-mail: info@emcdda.eu.int
Web site: www.emcdda.eu.int
Provides objective, reliable and comparable information on drugs.

The Florence Nightingale Hospital
11-19 Lisson Grove
London, NW1 6SH
Tel: 020 7258 3828
Fax: 020 7724 6827
Web site: www.florencenightingalehospitals.co.uk
Specialises in the treatment of psychological and emotional problems and addictions.

Hope UK
25f Copperfield Street
London, SE1 0EN
Tel: 020 7928 0848
Fax: 020 7401 3477
E-mail: enquiries@hopeuk.org
Web site: www.hopeuk.org
Provides education and training for parents, churches and voluntary youth organisations.

International Narcotics Control Board (INCB)
Vienna International Centre
Room E-1339, PO Box 500
A-1400 Vienna, Austria
Tel: + 43 1 26060 5482
Fax: + 43 1 26060 5867
E-mail: secretariat@incb.org
Web site: www.incb.org
The independent control organ for the implementation of the United Nations drug conventions.

Libertarian Alliance
25 Chapter Chambers
Easterbrooke Street
London, SW1P 4NN
Tel: 020 7821 5502
Fax: 020 7834 2031
E-mail: admin@libertarian.co.uk
Web site: www.libertarian.co.uk
Campaigns for civil and economic liberties.

Libra Project
205 Cowley Road
Oxford, OX4 1XA
Tel: 01865 245634
Fax: 01865 244970
E-mail: libra-project@mailbase.ac.uk
Web site: www.brookes.ac.uk/health/libra/index.html
Offers free and confidential information and counselling to

anyone who feels they have a problem around alcohol or drugs.

The Maranatha Community
102 Irlam Road, Flixton,
Manchester, M41 6JT
Tel: 0161 748 4858
Fax: 0161 747 7379
Web site: www.maranathacommunity.org.uk
Work to become more effective Christians in life, work and worship.

National Centre for Social Research
35 Northampton Square
London, EC1V 0AX
Tel: 020 7250 1866
Fax: 020 7250 1524
E-mail: info@natcen.ac.uk
Web site: www.natcen.ac.uk
The largest independent social research institute in Britain.

Release
388 Old Street
London, EC1V 9LT
Tel: 020 7729 5255
Fax: 020 7729 2599
E-mail: info@release.org.uk
Web site: www.release.org.uk
Provides a range of services dedicated to meeting the health, welfare and legal needs of drugs users. 24-hour helpline on 020 7729 9904.

Transform Drug Policy Institute (TDPI)
Easton Business Centre, Felix Road
Easton, Bristol, BS5 0HE
Tel: 0117 941 5810
Fax: 0117 941 5809
E-mail: info@transform-drugs.org.uk
Web site: www.transform-drugs.org.uk and www.tdpi.org.uk
The leading independent UK organisation campaigning for a just and effective drug policy.

Turning Point
New Loom House, 101 Backchurch Lane, London, E1 1LU
Tel: 020 7702 2300
Fax: 020 7702 1465
E-mail: tpmail@turning-point.co.uk
Web site: www.turning-point.co.uk
A social care organisation working with individuals in the areas of drug and alcohol misuse.

INDEX

ACKNOWLEDGEMENTS

The publisher is grateful for permission to reproduce the following material.

While every care has been taken to trace and acknowledge copyright, the publisher tenders its apology for any accidental infringement or where copyright has proved untraceable. The publisher would be pleased to come to a suitable arrangement in any such case with the rightful owner.

Chapter One: Drug Misuse

Young make drugs part of everyday life, © Guardian Newspapers Limited 2003, *Drugs identification guide*, © Metropolitan Police, *How many drugs are seized by customs and the police?*, © DrugScope, *Drug use among people in England*, © National Centre for Social Research/National Foundation for Educational Research, *Prevalance of drug misuse*, © Crown copyright is reproduced with the permission of Her Majesty's Stationery Office, *Drug misuse*, © Florence Nightingale Hospitals, *Drug use in Europe and its consequences*, © European Monitoring Centre for Drugs and Drug Addiction (EMCDDA), *Recent use of cocaine and cannabis*, © European Monitoring Centre for Drugs and Drug Addiction (EMCDDA), *Young cannabis users at more risk of mental illness*, © Telegraph Group Limited, London 2003, *Zero tolerance conceals drug use in schools*, © Guardian Newspapers Limited 2003, *Tackling young people's drug problems*, © Crown copyright is reproduced with the permission of Her Majesty's Stationery Office, *Drug proofing your kids*, © Care for the Family, *Drugs: what you should know*, © KidsHealth.org, *Risk reduction*, © The Libra Project, *Patterns of drug use among 16- to 59-year-olds*, © Crown copyright is reproduced with the permission of Her Majesty's Stationery Office, *New drugs strategy*, © Turning Point, *Tackling the drugs problem*, © Crown copyright is reproduced with the permission of Her Majesty's Stationery Office.

Chapter Two: Drugs and the Law

Getting into trouble with drugs, © DrugScope, *Britain's drug habit*, © Guardian Newspapers Limited 2003, *Drug laws*, © DrugScope, *Our fight against drug smuggling*, © Crown copyright is reproduced with the permission of Her Majesty's Stationery Office, *Your rights on arrest*, © Release, *Government to cut sentences for drug dealers*, © The Christian Institute, *The reclassification of cannabis*, © Cascade, *Cannabis among total of drug use/possession arrests*, © Reitox national reports/European Monitoring Centre for Drugs and Drug Addiction (EMCDDA), *Government proposals on cannabis*, © Crown copyright is reproduced with the permission of Her Majesty's Stationery Office, *The liberalisation of cannabis*, © The Maranatha Community, *Questions and answers about cannabis*, © Hope UK, *Legalising drugs will save lives*, © Transform Drug Policy Institute (TDPI), *Legalising cannabis would be a 'historical mistake'*, © International Narcotics Control Board, *Confusion on cannabis*, © The Daily Mail, February 2003, *What is effective drug policy?*, © Transform, *'Legalise all drugs now'*, © The Libertarian Alliance, *As long as drugs are illegal the problem won't go away*, © Guardian Newspapers Limited 2003, *Cannabis poll*, © MORI.

Photographs and illustrations:

Pages 1, 10, 18, 29: Pumpkin House; pages 6, 12, 23: Bev Aisbett; pages 9, 11, 13, 17, 24, 30, 32, 36: Simon Kneebone.

Craig Donnellan
Cambridge
May, 2003